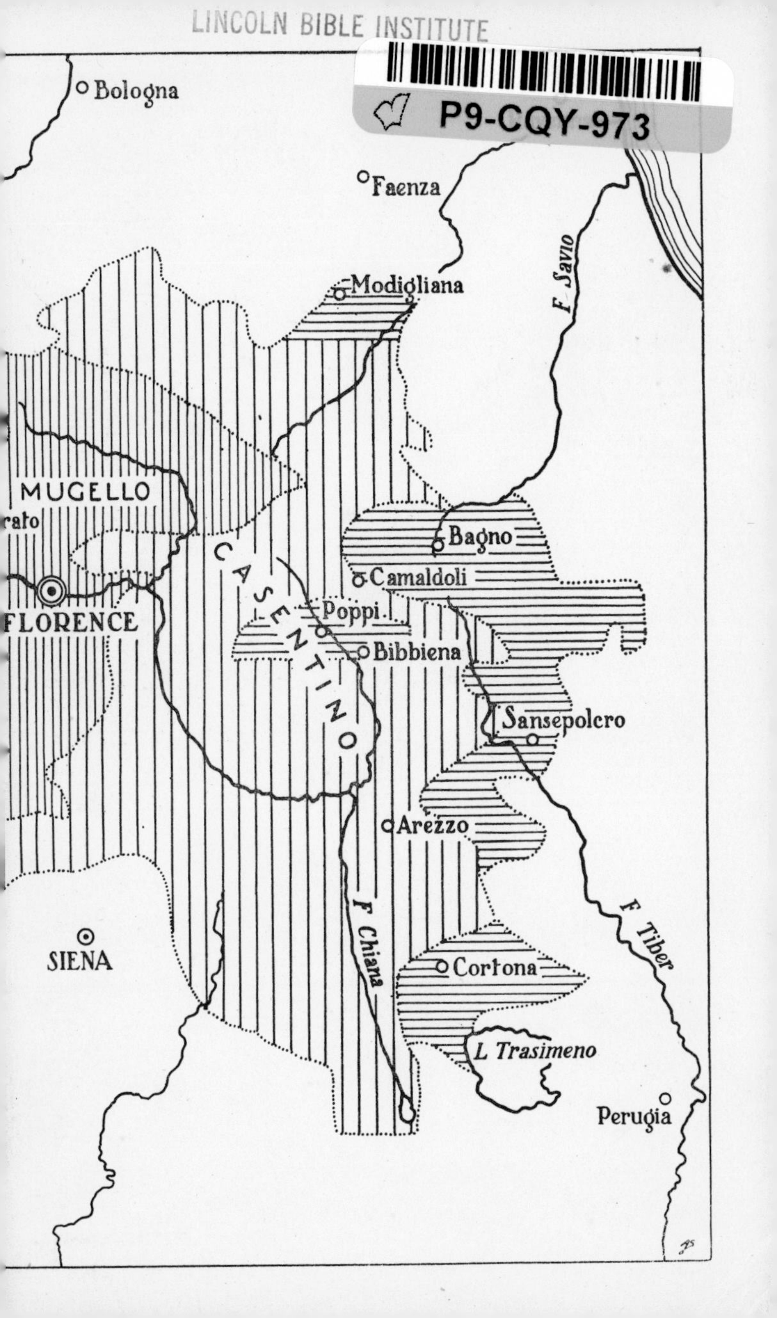
Bologna
Faenza
Modigliana
F Savio
MUGELLO
rato
FLORENCE
CASENTINO
Bagno
Camaldoli
Poppi
Bibbiena
Sansepolcro
Arezzo
F Chiana
F Tiber
Cortona
SIENA
L Trasimeno
Perugia

LORENZO DEI MEDICI

and

Renaissance Italy

is one of the volumes
in the
TEACH YOURSELF HISTORY
LIBRARY

Edited by A. L. ROWSE

Teach Yourself History

VOLUMES READY OR IN PREPARATION

The Use of History, by A. L. Rowse
Pericles and Athens, by A. R. Burn
Alexander the Great and the Hellenistic Empire, by A. R. Burn
Agricola and Roman Britain, by A. R. Burn
Constantine and the Conversion of Europe, by A. H. M. Jones
Charlemagne and Western Europe, by H. St. L. B. Moss
Wycliffe and the Beginning of English Nonconformity, by K. B. McFarlane
Henry V and the Invasion of France, by E. F. Jacob
Joan of Arc and the Recovery of France, by Alice Buchan
Lorenzo dei Medici and Renaissance Italy, by C. M. Ady
Erasmus and the Northern Renaissance, by Margaret Mann Phillips
Cranmer and the English Reformation, by F. E. Hutchinson
Whitgift and the English Church, by V. J. K. Brook
Raleigh and the British Empire, by D. B. Quinn
Richelieu and the French Monarchy, by C. V. Wedgwood
Cromwell and the Puritan Revolution, by Mary Coate
Milton and the English Mind, by F. E. Hutchinson
Louis XIV and the Greatness of France, by Maurice Ashley
Peter the Great and the Emergence of Russia, by B. H. Sumner
Chatham and the British Empire, by Sir Charles Grant Robertson
Cook and the Opening of the Pacific, by James A. Williamson
Catherine the Great and the Expansion of Russia, by Gladys Scott Thomson
Warren Hastings and British India, by Penderel Moon
Washington and the American Revolution, by Esmond Wright
Robespierre and the French Revolution, by J. M. Thompson
Napoleon and the Awakening of Europe, by F. M. H. Markham
Bolivar and the Independence of Spanish America, by J. B. Trend
Jefferson and American Democracy, by Max Beloff
Pushkin and Russian Literature, by Janko Lavrin
Abraham Lincoln and the United States, by K. C. Wheare
Napoleon III and the Second Empire, by J. P. T. Bury
Livingstone and Africa, by Jack Simmons
Gladstone and Liberalism, by J. L. Hammond and M. R. D. Foot
Clemenceau and the Third Republic, by J. Hampden Jackson
Woodrow Wilson and American Liberalism, by E. M. Hugh-Jones
Lenin and the Russian Revolution, by Christopher Hill
Botha, Smuts and South Africa, by Basil Williams
Gandhi and Modern India, by Guy Wint

LORENZO DEI MEDICI
and
Renaissance Italy

by

Cecilia M. Ady, D.Litt.

ENGLISH UNIVERSITIES PRESS LTD.

102, NEWGATE STREET

LONDON, E.C.1

FIRST PRINTED . . 1955

PRINTED AND BOUND IN ENGLAND
FOR THE ENGLISH UNIVERSITIES PRESS, LTD.,
BY HAZELL, WATSON AND VINEY LTD., AYLESBURY

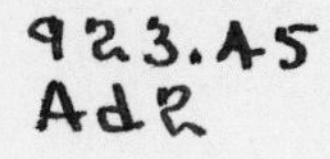

DEDICATION

To the pupils who for many years
have stimulated my studies in the
Italian Renaissance

Contents

ACKNOWLEDGMENTS

My thanks are due to Mr. Louis Marks for the new light thrown by his two unpublished theses on the finances of Florence under Lorenzo, and also for the loan of copies of the financial commissions set up in Florence in 1481 and 1491

A General Introduction to the Series

THIS series has been undertaken in the conviction that there can be no subject of study more important than history. Great as have been the conquests of natural science in our time—such that many think of ours as a scientific age *par excellence*—it is even more urgent and necessary that advances should be made in the social sciences, if we are to gain control of the forces of nature loosed upon us. The bed out of which all the social sciences spring is history; there they find, in greater or lesser degree, subject-matter and material, verification or contradiction.

There is no end to what we can learn from history, if only we would, for it is coterminous with life. Its special field is the life of man in society, and at every point we can learn vicariously from the experience of others before us in history.

To take one point only—the understanding of politics: how can we hope to understand the world of affairs around us if we do not know how it came to be what it is? How to understand Germany, or Soviet Russia, or the United States—or ourselves, without knowing something of their history?

There is no subject that is more useful, or indeed indispensable.

Some evidence of the growing awareness of this may be seen in the immense increase in the interest of the reading public in history, and the much larger place the subject has come to take in education in our time.

This series has been planned to meet the needs and demands of a very wide public and of education—they are indeed the same. I am convinced that the most congenial, as well as the most concrete and practical, approach to history is the biographical, through the lives of the great men whose actions have been so much part of history, and whose careers in turn have been so moulded and formed by events.

The key-idea of this series, and what distinguishes it from others that have appeared, is the intention by way of a biography of a great man to open up a significant historical theme; for example, Cromwell and the Puritan Revolution, or Lenin and the Russian Revolution.

My hope is, in the end, as the series fills out and completes itself, by a sufficient number of biographies to cover whole periods and subjects in that way. To give you the history of the United States, for example, or the British Empire or France, via a number of biographies of their leading historical figures.

That should be something new, as well as convenient and practical, in education.

I need hardly say that I am a strong believer in people with good academic standards writing once more for the general reading public, and of the public being given the best that the universities can provide. From this point of view this series is intended to bring the university into the homes of the people.

A. L. ROWSE.

ALL SOULS COLLEGE,
OXFORD.

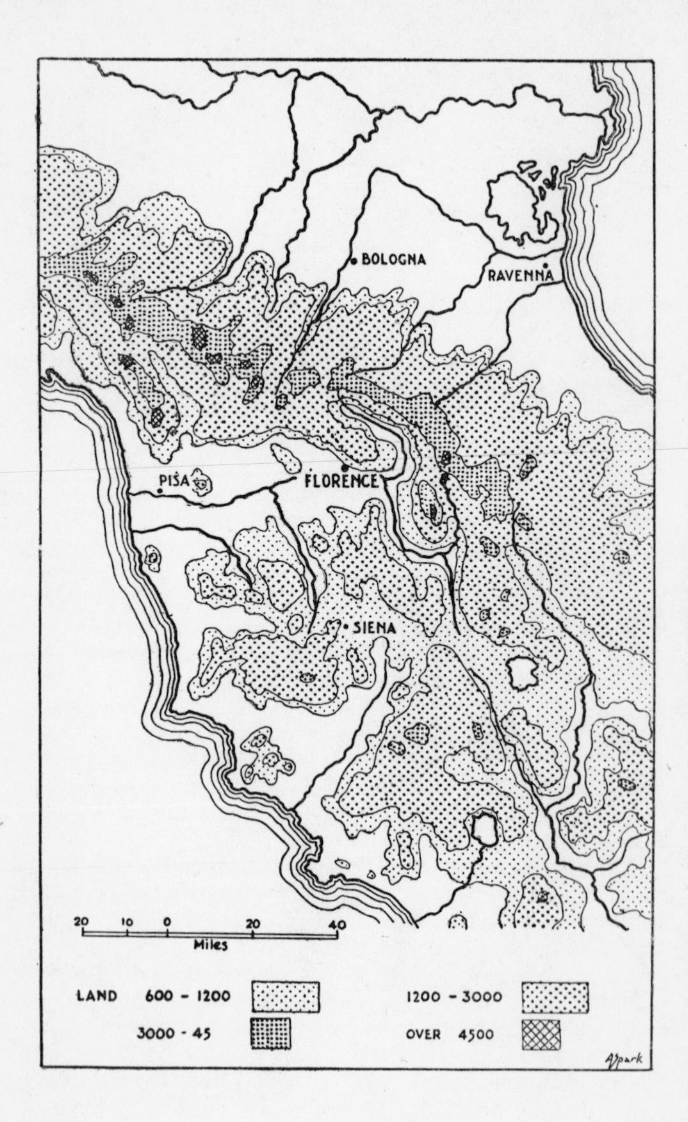
BOLOGNA
RAVENNA
PISA
FLORENCE
SIENA
20
10
0
20
40
Miles
LAND 600 - 1200
1200 - 3000
3000 - 45
OVER 4500

Chapter One

Introduction

"THERE was an Italian Renaissance whatever we may choose to call it." The words of C. J. Haskins give some idea of the nature of the controversy, which has not yet ended, as to the origins, the significance and the very existence of the Italian Renaissance. Nineteenth-century writers on the subject were impressed with the spirit of adventure which showed itself in every field of activity, with man's new-born confidence in his own powers, his enthusiasm for classical culture, his passion for beauty, his interest in the history of his own times and, above all, in his determination to make his mark in the world. Thus they depicted the Renaissance as essentially a new age, when men and women escaped from the shackles of mediæval tradition, when interests were concentrated on the blessedness of this life rather than on that of the world to come, and when to win fame became the goal of existence. From this new outlook arose the conviction that the classics rather than the Church could best teach men how to understand, enjoy and conquer the world in which they lived, and that in the pursuit of success moral restraints of every kind could be set aside.

All these characteristics of the Renaissance are true, but they are not the whole truth. Many that the nineteenth century looked upon as distinctive of the age have their origins far back in the civilization of mediæval Italy. From early times the Italians claimed to be the heirs of ancient Rome. Before the close of the eleventh century city-dwellers, in their efforts towards self-government, had enough classical learning and legal training to call their elected officers consuls and to look upon the Roman

Republic as their model. The classical tradition was never wholly lost, and in the course of the Middle Ages it was slowly recaptured. Italians of the fifteenth century were able to bring the ideals of the classical world to bear upon their art and their literature, their political and social life because, through the labours of scholars in collecting and editing texts and of archæologists in excavating ancient buildings and statuary, they had at last gained an adequate conception of the character of ancient civilization. If Italians had long revered the Roman world from which they had sprung, the men of the Renaissance recognized with pride the contribution to the art of living made by the mediæval city-state; its civilization was rooted in the Christian religion. When Dante wrote of Florence as the sheep-fold of San Giovanni, he expressed the love of the Florentines for their patron and protector, St. John Baptist. His feast was the hey-day of the year, when the city gave itself up to rejoicing. The care and maintenance of his church was the responsibility of the *Arte di Calimala*, the oldest of the Florentine trade-guilds, which before the end of the thirteenth century encased the Baptistery of San Giovanni in its familiar black-and-white marble. Here every Florentine child was brought for baptism. In Florence, as elsewhere, public and private wealth was spent on the building of churches and chapels, and the Christian story provided the theme for the artists who decorated them. Lent preachers in the principal church of the city were everywhere chosen by the civic authorities, and crowds came to listen both for instruction in their faith and in order to enjoy a feast of oratory. There were Renaissance scholars, frankly pagan in their outlook, who made it their aim to think, write and live as ancient Romans. The majority of Italians, reared in the traditions of the city-state, were less inclined to reject Christianity for paganism than to seek for a means of reconciling the classical system with the Christian.

Today the Middle Ages no longer appear to us as dark, and the Renaissance is seen to be in many ways rather the culminating point of mediæval civilization than a new beginning. Once more, however, this expresses only a half-truth. The differences between classical and Christian ways of life and thought were too great to be brought into harmony. The effort to do so caused a state of uncertainty in which old standards of faith and morals were undermined and nothing stable was put in their place. Everyone was left to make his own choice among the many alternatives presented to him—religion, politics, society, art and letters were all fields for experiment. So endless are the varieties which can be included under the term Renaissance that every attempt to pass judgment on the age is inadequate.

It is because of the varied and often conflicting elements in Renaissance Italy that Lorenzo dei Medici is its most representative figure. There are among his contemporaries men of more outstanding genius than he, yet their achievements belong to a limited sphere. As artist and scientist, Leonardo da Vinci's genius came nearest to realizing the ideal of universality, but he stood aloof from the political world which absorbed much of the thought and energy of the times. Niccolò Machiavelli is the unrivalled interpreter of the politics of his day, but his poems and his plays show hardly less plainly than *Il Principe* and the *Discorsi* that his preoccupation was always with statecraft. Lorenzo dei Medici's distinction lies in his ability to make his influence felt in every aspect of contemporary life. To his statesmanship Florence owed her golden age, when the city was at peace, trade prospered and all the arts flourished. As the head of the Medici bank, with business connexions throughout Europe, he directed Florentine commercial policy. His skilful diplomacy did much to preserve peace between the Italian states, and raised Florence to a position of influence out of all proportion to her strength. As one of the most gifted poets of the day, his place in artistic and literary circles was that of a fellow-worker rather than a patron. Voltaire writes of him as the ideal of an enlightened despot, yet he was not a prince but a citizen, taught from infancy to make the welfare of Florence his first consideration. He was at once a Platonist and a Christian, a student and a man of abundant physical energy, a town-dweller and a country-man who, like his grandfather Cosimo, could talk of farming as if he never did anything else but farm.

No one has been better loved or more hated. Historians of his own day and since have written of him on the one hand as a tyrant, vicious, bloodthirsty and self-seeking, and on the other hand as a man of peace, a good friend and a loyal citizen. He died at the age of forty-three, and his passing sealed the fate of the Medici ascendancy within the framework of the Florentine republic. For all that he achieved in his short life, he was not able to build for the future. Not long after his death Italy was held in the grip of foreign conquerors, and Florentine pre-eminence in the arts passed from a city weakened by faction and financial chaos to other centres of culture. In his failure as in his success, he is representative of his time. The Laurentian age in Florence, like that of the Renaissance in Italy, was as transitory as it was brilliant.

Chapter Two

The Rise to Power of the Medici

LORENZO DEI MEDICI was born on January 1, 1449, or according to Florentine reckoning, which began the year on Lady Day, January 1, 1448. At that time his grandfather Cosimo had made himself dominant in the Republic. His rise to power was the outcome of his skilful use of the peculiar conditions which prevailed in Florence. These are well described by Guicciardini, the greatest contemporary Italian historian, when he writes of the passion of the Florentines for equality coupled with the desire of every family to be first in the city. Liberty in Florentine eyes represented the highest good, and liberty meant both freedom from subjection to another state and a republican constitution under which every class in the city had its share of political responsibility. In pursuit of this ideal, the Florentines had fought successfully against Pope, Emperor and foreign princes who in turn had threatened their independence, and had frustrated every attempt on the part of one of their own citizens to set up a despotism.

The fact that Florence remained a republic at a time when most of the North Italian cities fell into the hands of despots is mainly due to her great merchant families—*Popolo Grasso* as they were called—whose commercial interests extended throughout the civilized world. Members of the *Popolo Grasso* were enrolled in one or other of the seven greater trade-guilds (*Arti*). Of these the *Arte di Calimala* had risen to prominence in the twelfth century first as importers and then as dressers and dyers of foreign cloth. In the fourteenth century the *Arte della Lana* brought the wool trade to its zenith, and, although in the

Medicean period it was overshadowed by the guild of silk merchants, it remained the largest employer of labour in Florence. The *Arte del Cambio* included all those engaged in the exchange of money, whether in local pawnbroking or in world-wide banking arising out of the network of Florentine commerce. The lawyers were employed to draw up trading contracts, and to protect the interests of the merchants both at home and abroad. Members of the *Arte dei Medici e Speziali* included both physicians and purveyors of dyes, drugs, spices and other products of the East. The skinners traded in leather-work, for which the Florentines still retain their ancient skill. No guild limited itself strictly to its special sphere, but all tended to deal indiscriminately in whatever profitable line of business came their way. Together, the Florentine merchants had, by their initiative, acumen and artistic gifts, unaided by any peculiar advantages of site or climate, built up a vast commercial and industrial system. They brought wool from England and Spain, dyes from the East and spun silk from Lombardy, which, together with their skill in manufacture and a highly organized banking system, enabled them to market Florentine cloth and silk in many lands.

If the members of the *Popolo Grasso* had been united among themselves they could have imposed their will upon Florence, but they were never free from dissensions. Business rivalries, family quarrels, political issues were among the perennial causes of disunity, and when a split in their ranks occurred other classes in Florence were prompt to take advantage of it. Butchers, bakers, shoemakers and other trades-people engaged in supplying the daily needs of the Florentines were organized in fourteen lesser guilds. They were represented in the *Signoria*, or chief magistracy, of the republic, but the majority of places belonged to the greater guilds, and the aim of the *Popolo Minuto* was always to increase their share in the government. The nobles were excluded from the *Signoria*, although socially there was little to distinguish them from the *Popolo Grasso*. They had houses in the city and in many cases a stake in commerce, whilst the merchants were landowners as well as they. Their political rights were, however, confined to that of eligibility for the *Consiglio del Comune* composed of representatives from the four quarters of the city, the other legislative council, the *Consiglio del Popolo*, being confined to members of the *Arti*. The consent of both councils was necessary before measures sent down from the *Signoria* became law, but although members could vote, they could not speak against any measure. It was inevitable that the nobles should resent so exiguous a share in political activities. Faction among the merchants often took the form of rival parties seeking to gain support from either the nobles or the trades-people by championing their grievances. Outside these three classes stood the artisans, whose political rights were limited to shouting their consent to changes in the constitution when the great bell rang out summoning all citizens to a *Parlamento* in the Piazza della Signoria. Disturbances which might have the effect of hampering their employers were never unwelcome to them.

In the later years of the fourteenth century a democratic revolution known as the rising of the Ciompi found supporters among both the greater and the lesser guilds. It won for the time being the right of association for the workers. Two new guilds were formed, of weavers and dyers, their members being made eligible for election to the *Signoria*; but a government hitherto conducted in the interests of a single class failed as an arbiter between employer and employed. A serious decline in trade paved the way for the suppression of the Ciompi and the triumph of the *Popolo Grasso*. From this time the merchant families found a means of preserving their solidarity by allowing one of their number to direct their policy. Under the leadership of first Maso and then Rinaldo d'Albizzi, members of a family of wool-merchants, Florence progressed in many spheres. The republic was the backbone of the resistance to the attempt of the Duke of Milan (Gian Galeazzo Visconti) to make himself supreme in Italy. Arezzo, Pisa and Livorno were added to Florentine territory. Trade flourished, and there was a remarkable outburst of intellectual and artistic activity within the city. After Maso's death (1417) harmony among the ruling class and their hold upon the government began to decline. Rinaldo lacked the qualities necessary to the maintenance of his authority, and the malcontents sought a champion in the person of a wealthy banker, Giovanni dei Medici.

The name of Medici is mentioned by Dino Campagni, the chronicler of Dante's Florence, who describes them in 1301 as "powerful citizens", members of the "Black" party, assaulting and wounding a "White" rival in a street fray. During the fourteenth century members of the family were chosen more than once as head of the Republic (*Gonfaloniere di Giustizia*), and are also found among the *Priori* who, with the *Gonfaloniere*, formed the *Signoria*. As, however, both offices were held only for two months, the distinction is not so great as it may appear. Salvestro dei Medici earned popularity for his name by supporting the cause of the Ciompi, and Giovanni, his distant kinsman, inherited the good-will of the populace. Giovanni's immediate ancestors owned a farm at Cafaggiolo in the mountainous district of Mugello, east of Florence, which was for long the country home of the Medici. From these small beginnings Giovanni built up a fortune which at the time of his death (1429) had made him one of the richest men in Italy. He helped to endow the Foundling Hospital of the Innocenti, and contributed to the building of San Lorenzo, soon to become the parish church of the Medici; there were few good causes in Florence that did not benefit from his generosity. He took such part in public life as his standing in the city required, serving on embassies and being elected to the *Signoria*. He became the spokesman of a party which drew support from the lesser guilds, and was opposed to the Albizzi policy of restricting the government to a narrow circle of their friends. The ruling faction made efforts to gain his co-operation, but he tried as far as possible to keep out of politics and to devote himself to his business as a banker.

On his death, his son Cosimo constituted himself the chief critic of the government. Soon afterwards an unsuccessful war with Lucca sounded the death-knell of the Albizzi supremacy. Rinaldo, in an attempt to make Cosimo a scapegoat for his own failure, caused him to be summoned to the Palazzo Vecchio and accused of various crimes. He and other members of his family were enemies of the republic who had tried repeatedly to seize power for themselves, and he had promoted the war with Lucca which brought disgrace upon Florence. With regard to the war, Cosimo had expressed doubts of the wisdom of embarking upon it, and his responsibility for pressing it was shared by many. Any pretext, however, served to provide a disgruntled government with a victim, and Cosimo was kept in prison while the *Signoria* debated on whether he should be executed or banished. Milder counsels prevailed, and he was exiled to Padua for ten years. His enemies trusted that he would suffer not only political eclipse but bankruptcy through inability to attend to his business in Florence. Here the banking connexions of his firm came to his aid. Padua lay within Venetian territory, and his relations with Venice were intimate. Through the intercession of the Venetian government his place of exile was transferred from Padua to Venice, where he was received as an honoured guest, and was able to carry on his work. Meanwhile opposition to Rinaldo in Florence increased, and after a year in exile Cosimo was recalled by a newly elected *Signoria*. In October 1434 Cosimo returned to Florence, amid the acclamations of his fellow-citizens; from that time until his death in 1464 he was ruler of the city in all but name.

Cosimo's sole title to rule in Florence was the consent of his fellow-citizens. Three times during his ascendancy he was elected *Gonfaloniere di Giustizia* for the normal period of two months; thus he was the legal head of the Republic for six months only in the course of thirty years. He had throughout to convince the Florentines that his leadership was in the best interests of the city. On the one hand he must maintain a strong and united government; on the other hand, he must preserve intact the forms of a republic. Rinaldo d'Albizzi died in exile because he failed in this exacting task. Cosimo, wiser and less scrupulous than he, retained and increased his power. Supreme authority lay with the *Signoria*, elected by lot from among those eligible for office, the *Gonfaloniere* and six *Priori* being members of the greater guilds, and the two remaining *Priori* belonging to the lesser guilds. Cosimo's control over the state required that each bi-monthly election should produce a chief magistracy composed of his friends. One means to this end was to use the opportunity afforded by the periodical revision of the election bags in order to exclude untrustworthy names. Elections to the *Signoria* were hedged about with an elaborate set of qualifications and disqualifications; one man might be rejected because he had not paid his taxes or because he was accused of a political offence, another because he was too young to qualify or because he or a near relation had recently held office. All these were weapons in the hands of a committee of Mediceans charged with the work of revision.

In times of emergency the consent of *Parlamento* could be obtained for suspending elections and creating a temporary committee (*balia*) with power to nominate the *Signoria* during a given period. This method proved less clumsy than manipulation of the bags, and on one pretext or another consent was usually obtained for the creation of a new *balia* when the previous period of emergency expired. In 1459, Cosimo's opponents secured a brief return to the system of election by lot, but this was followed by the institution of the Council of a Hundred, composed of Medicean supporters, which had precedence over the older councils in legislation, and appointed a committee to nominate the *Signoria*. From this time little more was heard of election by lot until the fall of the Medici.

Nevertheless, the continued subservience of the *Signoria* to the will of Cosimo required a large body of his supporters in the city from which selection could be made. His ability to win and keep his ascendancy over members of all classes was the foundation of his success. Merchants gained commercial advantages from association with the Medici firm, and new friends among the *Popolo Grasso* were obtained by raising certain families from the lesser to the greater guilds. On the other hand, opponents were banished or ruined by taxation. It was Cosimo's policy to avoid bloodshed or open attack on prominent citizens. Neri Capponi, for example, who distinguished himself in the Florentine victory over the Milanese at Anghiari (1440), retained his independence, and was to the end of his life a popular and influential figure in the city. Another hero of Anghiari, the *condottiere* Baldaccio, was summoned to the Palazzo Vecchio on a charge of treachery, and murdered by being thrown from the window. This exceptional act of violence was perhaps a warning to Capponi to take note from the fate of his friend of the dangers of forfeiting Cosimo's good-will. The positive aspect of Cosimo's work for Florence is seen in the unwonted peace and prosperity which the exorcism of the curse of faction brought to the city.

Even more important is the increased prestige of Florence among other Italian states owing to the new direction which Cosimo gave to foreign policy. During the first half of the fifteenth century, the chief Italian states had been constantly at war. In Naples, a long succession war preceded the establishment of Alfonso, King of Aragon, on the throne. From the return of Pope Martin V to Rome, after the ending of the Great Schism, the papacy, bent on recapturing its authority in the states of the Church, struggled against the powerful Roman baronage and the local lords who had seized power in

Romagna. Venice and Florence fought together against Filippo Maria Visconti of Milan, who in the reconstruction of his father's dominion threatened to make himself master of Lombardy. When Visconti died in 1447, the frontiers of Venice had been advanced to include cities as far west as Brescia and Bergamo, and her armies stood within striking distance of Milan. It seemed to the Florentines that they had gained little from the common effort, and that the lion's share of the profits had gone to the Venetians, who were now a greater threat than Milan to their own freedom of action.

During the war Cosimo made friends with the great *condottiere*, Francesco Sforza, when he was fighting on the side of Venice. Now Sforza claimed the Duchy of Milan on the grounds of his marriage to Visconti's daughter, and Cosimo decided to help him to secure his throne. Cosimo recognized Sforza's qualities both as a soldier and a statesman, and he believed that if he held Milan he would be able to prevent Venetian domination of the Lombard plain and also to guard the passes of the Alps against foreign invaders. For three years Francesco fought, first in the service of the Ambrosian Republic set up in Milan, then on the side of Venice, and finally against both powers combined, receiving throughout diplomatic and financial support from Florence. There were murmurs among the Florentines on the desertion of a sister republic and on money spent in the cause of a would-be despot, but Cosimo's will prevailed. After Sforza had been proclaimed Duke, Florence and Milan entered into a formal alliance, and Florentine troops took part in the war against Venice and Naples which dragged on until peace was signed at Lodi in 1454. Sforza was now recognized as Duke of Milan by the Italian powers and Venice had gained only one city as the result of a seven years' war. The peace was followed by a league of all the chief states, formed with the twofold object of preventing its members from attacking their neighbours and presenting a united front against foreign aggression. The moment was favourable as the taking of Constantinople by the Turks (1453) had stressed the need for unity at home, but the co-operation between Cosimo and Sforza was the main factor which brought the Italian League of 1455 into being.

It needed all Cosimo's tact to reconcile the Florentines to the new system of alliances. Their ancient friendship with France was cemented by strong commercial ties, and it had been their policy to champion the claims of princes of the House of Anjou to Naples. Now Alfonso of Aragon was their ally, and they were pledged to refuse help to his Angevin opponents. Yet the danger of French invasion was real, and threatened Milan as well as Naples. Charles, Duke of Orleans, was the son of Valentina Visconti, and his claims had already been put forward. The habit of calling in French princes to take part in Italian quarrels was a grave danger to national independence. To Florence, militarily weak and dependent on her commerce, peace was of the first importance. So the policy of friendship between the Italian states was accepted in her own interests as well as in those of Italy. It did not break her alliance with France, but henceforth friendly relations between the two powers were used to dissuade the French from embarking on Italian adventures. The maintenance of the League and the principles which inspired it became identified with the Medici, and was pursued amid many setbacks and some measure of success as long as their ascendancy lasted. It fell to Lorenzo to continue and develop the lines of foreign policy laid down by his grandfather.

As his father before him, Cosimo was generous with his money. He spent large sums in charity and entertained lavishly. He contributed from his private means to public finance, built churches and monasteries, patronized the arts and was himself a devotee of learning. The first public library in Florence, built by Michelozzo to house the books bequeathed to Cosimo by the humanist Niccolò Niccoli, is a testimony both to his beneficence and to his tastes. His greatest contribution to the intellectual life of

Florence was the part which he played in furthering Platonic studies. This hard-headed business-man was also a mystic who at intervals in his crowded life retired to his private cell at the convent of St. Marco "to cultivate his soul". Platonism offered a clue to his questionings, and Marsilio Ficino was trained at his expense to become the head of his new Platonic Academy in Florence. "Come quickly," he wrote to Marsilio as he lay dying, "and bring with you the book *De summo bono* of our Plato. . . . I desire nothing more ardently than to know the road which best leads to felicity." After Cosimo's death, Marsilio wrote a letter to his young pupil Lorenzo extolling the virtues of the patron to whom he owed so much. Cosimo, he said, was devout towards God, just towards man. He was hard-working and careful with regard to his business, still more so in the affairs of the Republic; he was acute in argument, strong and wise in government; as greedy of time as Midas was of gold, he counted the hours of each day with the utmost precision, and throughout his life found a place for the study of philosophy. "Do you, my Lorenzo," the letter concludes, "continue, as you have begun, to fashion yourself according to the Idea of Cosimo." During Cosimo's later years, his fellow-citizens placed increasing trust in his judgment, having learned in the course of his leadership how often his policy had proved right. The ruthlessness and lack of scruple with which he had swept obstacles from his path were forgotten in the light of the services which he had rendered to Florence. At his death a grateful Republic ordered that the words "Pater Patriæ" should be written on his tomb.

Chapter Three

Lorenzo's Education

AT the time of Lorenzo's birth the family mansion in the Via Larga, built for his grandfather by Michelozzo, was approaching completion, and here his early years were spent. Cosimo had rejected the plans submitted to him by Brunelleschi in favour of Michelozzo's simpler design, on the ground that the former were too ostentatious for the house of a private citizen. Yet the Medici Palace was an imposing structure, with its courtyard and garden and its wide staircase leading to the *piano nobile*, and it was spacious enough to house three generations.

It was among a large and united family circle that Lorenzo received his first lesson in the art of living. Piero il Gottoso, the elder of Cosimo's two sons and Lorenzo's father, was, as his nickname shows, afflicted by the family ailment of gout. He was obliged to live a semi-invalid life, and found his chief pleasure in classifying and adding to the collection of manuscripts, jewels, cameos, vases and other antiques which became the glory of the Medici Palace. He was an affectionate if somewhat austere father, holding before Lorenzo his own high standard of duty and taking pains to see that his heir was not spoiled. His younger brother Giovanni is one of the most attractive personalities of the age. Handsome, gifted and companionable, he threw himself eagerly into every aspect of Florentine life and had many devoted friends. His death in 1463, coming shortly after that of his little son Cosimino, cast a shadow over Cosimo's last days.

For the child Lorenzo the most important members of the family were his grandmother and his mother—Contessina dei Bardi and Lucrezia Tornabuoni. Both came from wealthy merchant houses, but otherwise they represented two diverse types of Florentine womanhood. Contessina was the complete housewife; her preoccupations were the health of her husband, children and grandchildren and the state of their wardrobes, the making of oil and cheese, the bleaching of linen on the Medici farms, and the transport of the family bedding from one villa to another. Such are the topics which fill her letters. Lucrezia belonged to a new generation, whose interests spread beyond the family. She was the friend and patron of scholars and herself a writer of verse. The Tornabuoni were closely associated with the Medici in business and politics, and Lucrezia played her part in both. She even embarked on a business enterprise of her own—buying the sulphur springs of Morba from the Republic and turning them into a flourishing health resort. Her intelligence, her literary tastes and, not least, her deep piety made her a formative influence in her son's life. Until her death in 1482 she was to him "the counsellor who took many a burden off me". Lorenzo's only brother, Giuliano, was four years his junior, and he had three sisters, who may have been in the mind of Benozzo Gozzoli when he introduced into his glowing frescoes of the Procession of the Magi in the Medici private chapel three pretty girls on horseback all dressed alike with a tall feather in their caps.

An adjoining house in the Via Larga was occupied by Pierfrancesco dei Medici, the son of Cosimo's only brother Lorenzo. It is typical of the solidarity of the family that their father Giovanni left no will, and that his entire property passed to the two brothers jointly. Lorenzo had shared Cosimo's exile and was devoted to him, so that as long as he lived, and during the minority of his son, the two branches of the family worked together as one. When Pierfrancesco came of age, however, the property was divided according to an award made by some prominent citizens, and from that time relations between the cousins became less harmonious. Later, Lorenzo wrote rather bitterly in his *Ricordi* that Pierfrancesco got the best of the bargain—the more valuable things being assigned to him, and his interest of one-third in the family business being free from all expenses. Although ill-feeling persisted, the ancestral estate at Cafaggiolo remained the property of the whole family, and Pierfrancesco's two sons shared in the common life.

Lorenzo's education began at the age of five, his first tutor being Gentile Becchi, afterwards Bishop of Arezzo. A letter from Lucrezia to her husband describes her nine-year-old son busily learning the verses set him by his master and teaching them to his little brother. Three years later, when Piero was away from home, Becchi reported to him that Lorenzo "is well on with Ovid, and has read four books of Justinus". That the boy was no bookworm is seen from the remark : "Do not ask how he enjoys his studies. In all other matters he is obedient, and now you are away, the fear of transgressing makes him more diligent." The appointment of Argyropulos as Reader of Greek in the University in 1456 gave a new impetus to Hellenic studies; it was said that the young men whom he taught talked Greek so fluently that Florence might have been Athens. Lorenzo as he grew older was among the enthusiastic band of pupils who gathered round him. Two other distinguished men had an influential share in Lorenzo's education—Cristoforo Landino, one of the foremost Latin scholars of his day, and Marsilio Ficino, the Platonist. It was fortunate that these masters, each supreme in his own sphere, did not despise the vulgar tongue, but encouraged their pupil in his natural bent for Italian poetry. Both had a profound admiration for Dante—Landino wrote a commentary on the *Divina Commedia*, and Ficino at Lorenzo's request translated the *De Monarchia* into Italian from the Latin. At the same time, Lorenzo's own verse profited by Landino's dictum that a man must be a Latinist to write good Italian.

Classical studies were treated by humanist educators as the basis of a system which aimed at the development of man's entire personality, body, mind and spirit. Thus

Lorenzo's education was not confined to Greek and Latin. His day began by hearing Mass with his tutor, and at his mother's wish he was often taken to meetings of the confraternity of San Paolo, an association formed for common prayer and worship and the furtherance of good works among its members. He was taught to sing to his own accompaniment on the lyre, a form of music which commended itself to the times owing to the opportunities it gave for individual expression. Squarcialupi, the Cathedral organist, spoke warmly of his musical gifts, and Ficino describes him singing spiritual songs as if driven by a divine fury. To live in Florence in the middle of the fifteenth century was in itself an artistic education for a clever boy. The Cathedral, begun by Arnolfo di Cambio in 1296, was now crowned by Brunelleschi's dome, completed in the year of Cosimo dei Medici's return from exile. The development of sculpture could be traced from the work of Giotto on the Campanile and of Pisano on the first set of doors at the Baptistery, to Ghiberti's doors, named for their beauty "gates of Paradise", and the various statues by Donatello which adorned public and private buildings in the city. At the Church of Santa Maria del Carmine, Masaccio's frescoes gave a new impetus to Florentine painting comparable only to that made by Giotto a century earlier. The walls of the Convent of San Marco were covered with Fra Angelico's masterpieces of religious art. Nearly all that is best in Florentine art was there for the young Lorenzo to see. At home he could watch Benozzo Gozzoli at work in the chapel, and hear the talk of patrons and artists on all that was being done or contemplated in the city.

In appearance Lorenzo was tall and dark, with a sallow complexion, irregular features and flattened nostrils which deprived him of the sense of smell. This, he used to say, had its advantages as most smells were unpleasant. He was ugly, and at the same time dignified and possessed of great physical strength. He became an expert rider, and delighted in hawking and hunting. Many months of his boyhood were spent either at Cafaggiolo or at Careggi, a villa on the outskirts of Florence rebuilt for Cosimo by Michelozzo. During holiday seasons the whole family migrated to one of these country homes, and at other times the children would be sent there under the charge of a tutor. A glimpse of life at Cafaggiolo is given in a letter to Piero from his factor telling of some days spent by Lorenzo and Giuliano with their grandmother. On Sunday all three rode to Mass at a neighbouring convent, Contessina mounted on a mule belonging to Lorenzo. "The boys," ran the letter, "are very happy; they go out hawking and return in good time, and they keep the house and village alive." From sojourn at the Medici villas, Lorenzo gained the intimate acquaintance with country life and the love of nature which distinguish his poetry.

Within the Medici palace in Florence the standard of living conformed to the simple ways of a citizen family. Magnificence was reserved for the entertainment of guests, and to this the hosts contributed according to their age and capacity. When the heir to the Duchy of Milan stayed at Careggi in 1459 he noticed that Cosimo's second son, Giovanni, did not sit down to supper, as he was busy acting as steward of the feast. All, including the ten-year-old Lorenzo, assisted in the preparations, and after the meal Lucrezia and other ladies of the house gave an exhibition of Florentine dancing, assisted by some peasant girls. At a banquet given by the Republic to Leonora of Aragon on her bridal journey to Ferrara, after Lorenzo had succeeded to the first place in the city, he and his brother waited upon the guests. Florentine society knew no rigid class barriers and the younger citizens took their pleasures together. In winter boys and girls snow-balled each other in the streets, and the young men played Calcio, the Florentine equivalent of Rugby foot-ball. There were many practices before the great match in Carnival time, which attracted crowds of spectators. Later, Lorenzo's eldest son, Piero, proved a particularly good player. In summer there were picnic parties in the country, and at all seasons the young people danced and made love.

By the time Lorenzo was sixteen his name was already coupled with that of the eleven-year-old Lucrezia Donati. He wore her device in tournaments, and she became the inspiration of his poetry. Their relations were those of Dante and Beatrice, or Petrarch and Laura, rather than those of lover and mistress. Illicit sexual relations with the unmarried daughter of another leading Florentine family would have brought unwarrantable discredit upon the Medici. Lorenzo lived in an age when sins of the flesh were so much taken for granted as to make the Duke of Ferrara consider a portrait of his illegitimate daughter a suitable present to send to his fiancée, and a man of his immense vitality doubtless indulged his passions freely. Curiously enough, however, the only woman's name connected with him, save that of Lucrezia Donati, is Bartolomea dei Nasi, the wife of Donato Benci. For her, according to Guicciardini, he conceived at the age of forty a passionate attachment, going out to her villa at night and returning to Florence before dawn for the business of the day. Unlike most of his contemporaries, among them his grandfather and his brother, he acknowledged no illegitimate children. The obscurity which veils his amorous intrigues has given free play to the scandal-mongers of his own and later times. The most fantastic story comes from a nineteenth-century German historian who, misreading a reference to a consignment of fifty skins, all of the best quality, being sent to Lorenzo from Slavonia, announces that the order was for fifty Turkish slave girls, all very beautiful.

Lorenzo's training for public life began when he was fifteen, on the death of his grandfather. As the old man lay dying at Careggi, he congratulated himself that both his grandsons had good wits. Piero wrote to tell Lorenzo and Giuliano of Cosimo's last days, saying that the time had now come for them to "take up your share of the burden in good heart as God has ordained, and having been boys make up your minds to be men". During the next two years Lorenzo was sent on three missions. The first was to Pisa to meet Federico, the second son of King Ferrante of Naples, who was on his way to Milan to act as proxy for his elder brother, Alfonso, at his marriage with Ippolita Sforza. The visit was one of courtesy, and the chief subject of discussion between the two lads appears to have been the respective merits of classical and vernacular poetry. It bore fruit in Lorenzo's first literary effort, a letter on the Tuscan poets which he sent to Federico with a collection of their works. The friendship begun at Pisa lasted throughout Lorenzo's life. The next mission was to Milan, where Lorenzo was to represent his father at the wedding. On his way he visited Bologna, Venice and Ferrara, gaining an insight into Italian social and political life and also into the working of the Medici business. "This journey is the touchstone of your abilities," wrote his father, "show sense, industry and manly endeavour so that you may be employed in more important matters."

Bologna was a republic within the states of the Church, but its first citizen, Giovanni Bentivoglio, ruled over it as effectively as the Medici ruled in Florence. His family had close links with the Medici, and he looked to them to champion the independence of Bologna against attempts of the Papacy to establish direct rule over the city. Lorenzo was given a warm welcome there, as also in Venice, where the Medici had many business connexions. He was received by the Doge, and was able to satisfy his father that he had made nearly all the necessary calls on Venetian citizens. The Este of Ferrara were the oldest of Italian ruling families. Their court was renowned for its hospitality, and was a centre of gaiety and culture. So pressing was the invitation to stay longer in its congenial atmosphere that Lorenzo delayed his arrival in Milan. The Medici bank in Milan was a gift from Duke Francesco to Cosimo, and had been rebuilt and decorated by a Florentine architect. Its manager at this time was Pigello

Portinari, whose advice Lorenzo received instructions to follow in all that he did or said during his visit. Piero also told his son that if he entertained he need not spare expense, and that he must be careful not to give any trouble to the Duke, who would have enough on his hands with his daughter's wedding. From Milan Lorenzo hurried home to help in the preparations for entertaining the bridal party on its way to Naples. Ippolita Sforza at the age of fourteen had delighted Pope Pius II by the Latin oration which she addressed to him at the Congress of Mantua. Her literary tastes were a bond between herself and Lorenzo, and from the time of her stay in the Medici Palace they exchanged letters on topics of common interest. On one occasion Ippolita asked for a loan of 2,000 ducats, which she promised to repay on the word of an honourable woman.

Piero was satisfied that his son had done well enough on his Milanese mission to be entrusted with more important business, and in 1466 he was sent to Rome to negotiate with Paul II about a contract relating to the recently discovered alum mines at Tolfa. Alum was essential to the Florentine textile industry, as it was used for dyeing wool and silk in the most popular colours. Supplies hitherto had come chiefly from the Levant, and the concession which Lorenzo now obtained for the Medici to work the papal mines proved most profitable to them. Paul II had not long succeeded Pius II as Pope. The latter was a personal friend both of Cosimo and Francesco Sforza and a supporter of their peace policy, and Piero was apprehensive of the line which the new Pope would take. The death of Francesco Sforza, which occurred while Lorenzo was in Rome, was a further blow to the maintenance of peace. Lorenzo was told to do all he could to placate the Pope, and then to proceed to Naples, in order to make sure of the co-operation of the King in the event of any disturbance. He spent two months with his friends in Naples, and the favourable impression which

Ferrante gained of the character and abilities of his young guest was never lost.

Lorenzo returned to Florence to find a state of growing tension within the city which struck at the very foundations of his father's supremacy. Piero, owing to ill-health and a certain lack of geniality in his manners, was not so popular as Cosimo. Certain leading citizens considered that they had as good a right as the Medici to the first place in the government, and they took advantage of the death of the leader, whom all respected, to try to bring about a change. Among the malcontents was Luca Pitti, who had played an active part in political life under Cosimo and was now building himself a sumptuous palace on the south bank of the Arno. The others were Angelo Acciaiuoli, a member of a prominent merchant family, who had been disappointed in his hope of a Medici bride, and Diotisalvi Neroni, brother of the Archbishop of Florence, an able intriguer in whom Cosimo had shown misplaced confidence. With them was associated Niccolò Soderini, an idealist who pinned his hopes on the establishment of a genuinely democratic government in Florence. Piero's opponents won the first round of the battle, when, not long after Cosimo's death, they procured a return to the system of election by lot, which led to the choice of a *Signoria* unfavourable to the Medici, Soderini being elected *Gonfaloniere di Giustizia*. The new government could talk, but it could not act. Many plans were put forward and nothing was achieved. When the term of office of the reforming *Signoria* expired, a placard on the Palazzo Vecchio bearing the words "Nine fools are out" expressed the verdict of Florence upon its performance. Soderini was succeeded by a pro-Medicean *Gonfaloniere*, but the malcontents did not accept defeat, and in the summer of 1466 they took advantage of the state of Italy to obtain allies outside Florence for an attempt to achieve their ends by force.

The peace policy embodied in the Italian League placed a restraint upon political ambitions which was irksome to many. Venice was hindered in her aims of territorial expansion and the Papacy in its designs upon the states under its suzerainty. There were besides *condottieri* on the look-out for profitable wars, and French princes eager to press their claims. All these elements of unrest had been held in check by the strong hands of Francesco Sforza and Cosimo dei Medici, supported by the close alliance which they had formed with Naples. Now the Duke of Milan was young and inexperienced, and Piero dei Medici was an invalid. The moment seemed opportune for the overthrow of the Florentine government. Those who hatched the Neroni conspiracy were aware that their success would not be unwelcome either to Venice or to the Venetian Pope, Paul II, who had already shown signs of wishing to press his temporal claims more actively than his predecessor had done. It was agreed that Neroni and his friends should murder Piero when he was on his way back into Florence from Careggi, and that Borso d'Este should bring a troop of horse across the Apennines to assist the conspirators in taking possession of the city. Warning of trouble afoot had been given by Giovanni Bentivoglio, who had learned of Borso's movements. Thus when Lorenzo, who was riding in advance of his father's litter, saw a group of men gathered outside Archbishop Neroni's villa his suspicions were at once aroused. Asked whether Piero was on his way, he answered "Yes", and at once sent a messenger to warn the party to enter the city by another gate. Piero got home safely, and the presence of foreign troops outside the walls led to an outburst of loyalty among the citizens.

The conspirators, seeing that their cause was hopeless, yielded to the inevitable. With the flight of the archbishop and the banishment of practically all the members of the Neroni family, the hard core of resistance within Florence was eliminated. Niccolò Soderini and Angelo Acciaiuoli were sent into exile, but others of their name remained and gave their support to the Medici. Luca Pitti was left alone, to suffer complete eclipse in a city where his influence had been great. Such was his unpopularity that the workmen engaged in building his house laid down their tools. A *Parlamento* was summoned to approve a decree that election of the *Signoria* by lot should be suspended for ten years, and that a new *balia* should be set up with increased powers. Thus the control of the Medici over the government was strengthened, and the hereditary character of their supremacy was recognized by the provision that Lorenzo, although he was under age for office, should be allowed to represent his father on the *balia*, and also on the Council of a Hundred, which had to be consulted on all important affairs of State.

The last resort of Piero's opponents was the war of 1467. Bartolommeo Colleoni, a *condottiere* in Venetian service, was given leave of absence by Venice in order that he might serve her interests under cover of independent action. His plan, for which it was believed the Pope's consent had been obtained, was to make a descent upon Florence from Romagna in conjunction with the Florentine exiles. His designs were thwarted by the promptitude with which the friends of the Medici rallied to their defence. The young Duke of Milan came in person, and the Neapolitan contingent was headed by the heir to the throne. Federico, Duke of Urbino, was placed in command of the allied army. Giovanni Bentivoglio sent spies into Colleoni's camp, and kept the allies informed of his movements. Thus a descent of the enemy upon Tuscany was delayed, and the one battle of the war was fought at La Molinella in the neighbourhood of Bologna. Machiavelli asserts that not a single man was slain and only a few were wounded, but there were in fact considerable losses on both sides, and the Bolognese hospitals were filled with the wounded. The battle raged all day without decisive result, until as evening fell the fight was called off. In the spirit of *condottiere* warfare the two commanders shook hands and congratulated each other on coming unharmed out of the conflict. After this, Colleoni had no taste for further adventure; the troops withdrew into winter-quarters, and when peace was signed early in 1468, the long-drawn-out attempt to overthrow Piero's government was finally defeated.

During the war Lorenzo had remained in Florence, taking no part in the fighting. The Medici were not soldiers but business-men, and training in the profession of arms had no place in his education. Owing to his failing health, Piero grew increasingly reluctant to let his son out of his sight; without him, he complained, he was a man without hands. Since his grandfather's death Lorenzo had gained valuable experience of the nature of the task which lay before him when he became head of the family. He learned the closeness of the connexion between business and politics. One of the chief assets of the Medici in their relations with foreign powers was their position in the world of commerce, and their popularity in Florence was enhanced by the prestige which they enjoyed outside her walls. Whilst in the interests of the firm it was necessary to maintain control over both the economic and the foreign policy of the Republic, the events of the last few years had made plain how insecure were the foundations upon which the Medici supremacy rested. They had also shown the immense importance of winning trustworthy friends among Italian rulers. In order to maintain his supremacy and retain his allies, Lorenzo must keep his finger on the pulse of popular opinion, both at home and abroad. He had already shown that he possessed gifts which rendered him peculiarly fitted for the part he had to play, not least among them being the capacity for making friends in whatever company he found himself.

Chapter Four

Marriage and Call to Power

THE year 1469 was momentous for Lorenzo. In June he was married to Clarice Orsini; in December he succeeded on his father's death to the first place in the government. Marriage with the daughter of a Roman noble was a new departure for a member of the Florentine merchant oligarchy. Hitherto the Medici had conformed to the custom of their class and taken their wives from other wealthy citizen families. The marriage was not approved of in Florence, but it had advantages which commended it to Piero and Lucrezia. Clarice was the daughter of Jacopo Orsini of Monterotondo; and her mother, an Orsini of Bracciano, was the sister of Cardinal Latino, who was influential at the Papal Curia. The Orsini were soldiers by profession, and held large estates north of Rome, as well as in Neapolitan territory. An alliance with this powerful clan would offset the military weakness of Florence, give the Medici a hold over the Papacy and strengthen their existing ties with Naples. Piero was also aware that to choose his heir's bride within Florence would be to please one family and excite the envy of many.

It fell to Piero's brothers-in-law, Giovanni and Francesco Tornabuoni, who were in charge of the Medici bank in Rome, to take the necessary steps towards cementing the alliance, but before formal negotiations began Lucrezia went to Rome in order to see Clarice for herself. The report which she sent to her husband was favourable but by no means enthusiastic. Clarice, she said, had on first sight two good qualities, she was tall and fair; although not pretty, she had a good figure, a pleasing expression and a quantity of reddish hair. Her manners were not so attractive as those of the Florentine girls, and she did not, like them, carry her head proudly, but poked it forward a little. Her faults Lucrezia attributed to shyness, and she assured Piero that as their future daughter-in-law was very modest she would soon learn their ways. Altogether she was a girl much above the common, although she could not compare with their own three daughters. Making due allowance for maternal and patriotic prejudice, Lucrezia was probably right in her estimate that girls brought up in Florence were better educated and more fitted to take their place in society than one reared in the more conventional and secluded environment of an old feudal family. For all her noble birth, Clarice Orsini was no ideal mate for Lorenzo dei Medici. A few days later it was contrived that Lorenzo should get a glimpse of his proposed bride at Mass, and he expressed himself as content and ready to fall in with his father's wishes.[1] So in due course the contract was signed, Clarice's dowry being fixed at 6,000 florins in money, jewels and dresses. Both parties were well satisfied with the match, but the Orsini, far from looking upon it as a misalliance, were more eager for it than were the Medici.

Clarice was married by proxy in Rome, Filippo dei Medici, Archbishop of Pisa, acting on his kinsman's behalf. On February 7, 1469, the event was celebrated in Florence by a tournament of unsurpassed magnificence. Its story is told by Luigi Pulci, not as was long believed by his brother Luca, in a poem entitled *La Giostra di Lorenzo de' Medici*. The scene was the Piazza of Santa Croce, and there were eighteen competitors, a distinguished *condottiere*, Roberto da Sanseverino, being one of the judges. Pageantry on this occasion was of greater importance than feats of arms. Lorenzo entered the lists, preceded by trumpeters, drums and fifes, mounted on a

[1] Lucrezia's letters were written from Rome in March and April 1467.

horse given him by the King of Naples. His velvet cap was set with pearls, and on his shield was a great diamond known as *"Il Libro"*. Over his surcoat he wore a scarf embroidered with withered and blooming roses and a motto, *"Le temps revient"*, written in pearls. For the combat he exchanged his cap for a helmet surmounted by three blue feathers, and the charger which he rode was the gift of Borso d'Este. An honour of which Piero dei Medici was justly proud was the privilege granted by Louis XI to him and his heirs of bearing the royal arms of France. So Lorenzo entered the fray with the golden *Fleurs-de-lis* displayed on his shield.

Lorenzo's own account of the tournament written in his diary shows characteristic realism as to his part in the proceedings. "In order to do as others, I held a joust on the Piazza of Santa Croce, at great expense and with much pomp, on which I find about 10,000 ducats were spent. Although neither my years nor my blows were very great, the first prize was awarded to me, a silver helmet with Mars as its crest." Clarice, anxiously awaiting news of the tournament, feared so much for her betrothed's safety that she gave herself a headache, and on hearing of his success wrote him a stiff little letter of congratulation. The queen of the ceremonies, however, was not Clarice but Lucrezia Donati. Two years before, at a tournament given in celebration of a friend's wedding, Lucrezia gave Lorenzo a wreath of violets, and he promised to give an entertainment in her honour. At the *Giostra* held in her presence his promise was splendidly redeemed, and Lucrezia's smiles were the reward of victory. After this Lorenzo's passion appears to have cooled. Lucrezia was already married, and Clarice, accepting her as a friend of the family, became the godmother of her son.

Meanwhile the Tornabuoni brothers wrote letters from Rome in praise of Clarice in the hope of arousing Lorenzo's enthusiasm, and Cardinal Latino sent a pressing invitation to him to visit her. Perhaps through indifference on Lorenzo's part but more probably owing to

Piero's objection to his leaving Florence, the invitation was not accepted. When the time came, Giuliano dei Medici went in his brother's place to fetch the bride from Rome. In preparation for her coming the cities and villages of the Florentine dominion sent presents of meat, poultry, sweetmeats and wine to furnish the tables for the wedding feast. On Sunday morning, June 4, Clarice, who had arrived outside Florence overnight, made her way to the Medici Palace, where Lorenzo was awaiting her. Her dress was of white and gold brocade, and she rode the horse on which Lorenzo had entered the lists at Santa Croce. She was attended by a company of young men and girls, and on her arrival at the palace, in accordance with a Florentine custom, an olive tree was drawn up to the windows to the sound of music. There followed three days of feasting. Food and drink did not "exceed the modesty and simplicity suitable to a marriage"—there was never more than one roast, followed by sweetmeats such as marzipan and sugared almonds—but the setting of the banquets showed Florentine taste and ingenuity at their best. On the first day the bride and fifty young women dined in a loggia overlooking the garden whilst the bridegroom's mother entertained the older ladies on the balcony above. Tables for seventy senior citizens were spread under the arches of the courtyard, and the younger men dined in the hall. Great copper coolers were placed round Donatello's statue of David on its column in the centre of the courtyard and round the fountain in the garden; from these Tuscan wines were served to the guests. The table-cloths were of the finest damask, and each dish was brought in to the sound of trumpets. After dinner there was an interval for rest, and then the company reassembled to listen to music and watch the dancing performed on a stage hung with rich tapestries and with curtains embroidered with the Medici and Orsini arms. Conspicuous among the bride's presents was a Book of Hours, written in letters of gold on blue vellum with a binding worked in crystal and silver, the gift of

Lorenzo's first tutor, Gentile Becchi. Monday's festivities were spoiled by rain, but it cleared up on Tuesday, when the day began with Mass at San Lorenzo, and all the company wore their best clothes.

Lorenzo's union with Clarice Orsini was, as he recognized, a *mariage de convenance*, but it was not other than happy. Family ties among the Medici were sacrosanct, and when Clarice became one of themselves Lorenzo treated her with kindness and consideration. She, however, had no taste either for art or literature, and knew nothing of politics; thus she was excluded from the main interests of Lorenzo's life, and was incapable of sharing in his cares and pleasures. A few weeks after the wedding Lorenzo went to Milan to stand godfather in Piero's place to the Duke's first-born son. The two short letters which he wrote to his wife, full of affection and bereft of news, are typical of their mutual relations. In the first he announces that he has arrived safely and is well: "This I think will please you better than any other news save that of my return, judging by my own longings for you and for home. Be good company to Piero, Mona Contessina and Mona Lucrezia, and I will soon come back to you. . . . Pray God for me, and if you want anything from here let me know before I leave. Your Lorenzo." Two days later he holds out prospects of a speedy return and tells Clarice to take care of herself.

Clarice gave birth to ten children, of whom three died in infancy and three sons and four daughters survived. Her rare letters to her husband are chiefly concerned with the health of herself and her family, or with commending her favourite preachers to Lorenzo's notice. Only one serious disagreement between them is recorded. This arose from Clarice's quarrels with Poliziano, the children's tutor, when they were all at Cafaggiolo during the war of 1478–9 and Lorenzo remained at his post in Florence. Clarice insisted that little Giovanni should learn to read Latin from the Psalter, instead of from the classical texts which Poliziano had chosen for him, and a few weeks later she drove the tutor from the house. Lorenzo's sympathies were all with his friend and fellow-poet, and although he acquiesced in his dismissal, he allowed him to live in his own room at Fiesole, which, Clarice complained, turned her into ridicule. Finally Lorenzo wrote expressing his annoyance that Clarice had not done as he had asked and sent Poliziano's books after him, and ordering that they should all be sent that evening without fail. As time went on Clarice became consumptive, and when she died in 1488, Lorenzo showed genuine grief at her loss. Her place in history is judged rightly by the Ferrarese ambassador, when he wrote to his master that Mona Clarice had died three days ago, but that he had not sent the news at once as it did not seem to him of much importance.

The last months of Piero dei Medici's life were overshadowed by anxiety. He had not recovered from the shock of the Neroni conspiracy, and he feared that his own death would be the signal for another attempt against the Medici supremacy. Fresh trouble was also brewing in Romagna, where Paul II took advantage of the death of Sigismondo Malatesta, Lord of Rimini, to claim the city as a lapsed fief. Venice promised her support, in the hope that Rimini might fall to her share, and when Sigismondo's son Roberto was recognized as lord by the citizens, papal and Venetian forces were sent to dislodge him. If Rimini fell, the fate of all Romagna would be in jeopardy, and Venice and the Papacy might be encouraged by the exiles to turn their arms against Florence in an attempt to wrest the government from Piero's dying hands. It was imperative that Florence and Milan should rally in Roberto's defence, and Lorenzo's invitation to the Sforza court seemed to offer a good opportunity for discussing what could best be done. It was only with great reluctance that Piero allowed his son to accept. His objection was not only to his leaving Florence, but to the possibility of his taking too much authority upon himself. From Careggi he wrote a petulant letter to his wife exhorting her to tell Lorenzo that he was not an ambassador and must not exceed his orders. "I am determined," he added, "that the gosling shall not lead the gander to drink." In Milan Lorenzo made himself, as usual, generally popular. He was careful to leave politics to be discussed through the normal diplomatic channels, and the magnificent gold and diamond necklace which he presented to the Duchess caused such delight that the Duke asked him to stand godfather to all his children. Meanwhile Roberto Malatesta, encouraged by the knowledge that he was not friendless, inflicted a defeat on the papal forces which caused Paul II's purpose to weaken, and the crisis over Rimini ended for the time being.

On December 2, Piero died at Careggi at the age of fifty-three. During the five years of his supremacy ill-health prevented him from being constantly in the public eye, and in consequence his hold over the Florentines weakened. His reputation has suffered at the hands of historians from the fact that he was preceded by a great father and followed by a brilliant son. Owing to these disadvantages his "worth and goodness", as Machiavelli notes, have not been fully recognized. Among his outstanding merits is his perception of the nature of his position in Florence. He was careful to act always through the organs of the republican constitution, and refrained from any attempt to make himself a dictator. Machiavelli's story that at the time of his death he was proposing to heal discontents among the Florentines by recalling all the exiles is typical of his patriotism and his readiness to forgive. In foreign affairs he continued and developed his father's policy, striving to keep the peace in Italy, and strengthening the friendship of Florence with Milan and Naples upon which peace depended. Louis XI of France was not alone among contemporary rulers in the tribute which he paid to Piero's wisdom, loyalty and perseverance. The inheritance upon which Lorenzo entered owed much to his father's quiet caretaking.

Lorenzo's unchallenged succession to supremacy was brought about by the prompt action of Tommaso Soderini, who had remained a faithful friend of the Medici throughout the efforts of his brother Niccolò to unseat them. Summoning about six hundred leading citizens to the Convent of Sant' Antonio, he spoke with all the eloquence at his command on the benefits which Cosimo and Piero had conferred on Florence and on the virtues of the two young men Lorenzo and Giuliano, who, he said, were as anxious as their father and grandfather had been to merit the good opinion of their fellow-citizens. Others took up the theme—among them members of the Pitti family—stressing the need for a head of the state in order to ensure unity in the conduct of public affairs. Thus it was with the unanimous consent of the meeting that Tommaso, accompanied by representatives of the ruling faction, came to the Medici Palace on the second day after Piero's death, and invited Lorenzo to assume the first place in the government. "The proposal being contrary to the instincts of my age and involving heavy burdens and dangers," wrote Lorenzo in his diary, "I accepted with reluctance, and only in order to safeguard our friends and our fortunes, for it is ill-living in Florence without control over the government."

Lorenzo was under no illusions with regard to the heaviness of the task which lay before him. He was now the head of a great banking firm with agents in distant branches looking to the home office for direction. In Florence he would find himself at the beck and call of everyone with ambitions or a grievance, as he could not afford to allow any section of the community to grow dissatisfied with his rule. He would have to deal with a vast diplomatic correspondence, studying the reports of envoys, giving them further instructions, writing personal letters to the heads of other states. All this was tedious work for a young man not yet one and twenty, who knew so many more agreeable ways of passing his time. He had devoted friends to help him, but because his power was unofficial, few of his responsibilities could be delegated. Yet he had been trained for the task from his infancy, and its very difficulties had their attraction for one conscious of his own exceptional abilities.

Chapter Five

The Medici Bank

IT was once held that the red balls (*palle*) figuring on the Medici coat-of-arms were a play on their name and represented a physician's pills. They are more probably connected with a pawnbroker's balls. The coat-of-arms of the *Arte del Cambio* was a red shield bearing golden balls. Thus balls came to be the symbol of trading in money, and may have suggested both the six red *palle* of the Medici arms and the three golden balls of the pawnbrokers' sign. The word *banco* in Florence was applied to undertakings varying from the city pawnbroking establishments to enterprises dealing in merchandise and exchange on a vast scale. Humble money-changers at work in the Florentine market belonged to the same guild as the Medici, whose business house is described by Philippe de Commynes as the greatest in the world. The Medici bank reached its peak under Cosimo, and when Lorenzo became head of the firm many persons in many places were trafficking under the sign of the *palle* "in the name of God and good fortune". From 1414 to 1476 the Medici were bankers to the Papacy, a position which brought them profitable business of a very varied kind. Medici agents were employed to search for classical texts or to engage singers for the papal choir. Collectors of papal taxes abroad would hand over their money to the nearest Medici bank. It might be used in the first instance to pay for the purchase of goods, as for instance a consignment of English wool destined for the *Arte di Lana* in Florence, and by means of bills of exchange find its way to Rome. The Medici bank received papal bulls appointing new bishops, which they held until the nominee had paid them his dues and returned to the Curia if these were not forthcoming. Sometimes this provided an opportunity to assist a particular candidate to obtain the see, as may be seen from a letter written in 1448 from Bruges to John Kemp, Cardinal Archbishop of York. Kemp wanted the Bishopric of London for his nephew Thomas, and the Bruges firm, writing to tell him that the bull was in their hands and asking that the dues might be paid to the Medici bank in London without delay, added that their colleagues in Rome had laboured to secure the prize against a rival supported by the King. In this case they did not labour in vain, as Thomas Kemp was Bishop of London for nearly forty years.

The Milanese bank was founded by Cosimo after Francesco Sforza became Duke; the latter made its manager his minister of finance, and the bank became an important centre of Medici business. In 1466 the bank at Geneva was transferred to Lyons; its extension under Lorenzo marked the increasingly friendly relations between himself and Louis XI. Here Philippe de Commynes had a deposit upon which he drew in order to have the necessary money to purchase his release from the iron cage in which he was imprisoned after Louis XI's death. Florence never succeeded in her efforts to develop a carrying trade of her own adequate to her needs. Thus the Medici bank in Venice continued to be the centre of Florentine trade with the East. When in the early fifties Florence and Venice were at war, the property of the bank was seized, but the business connexion was too valuable to all concerned to suffer more than a temporary rupture. Pisa was important for its trade with Spain, and the Medici bank there had agents in Valencia and Barcelona. The bank at Bruges had a long and interesting history, and it was closely linked with the London house. Among other branches were those of Avignon and Lübeck, although the latter was closed before Lorenzo's day.

Each branch formed a separate company with its own manager who was also a partner in the firm, but the

Medici retained control of the business by keeping more than half the shares in the hands of members of the family. Under the manager were factors and juniors known as *giovani*. Many a young Florentine owed his start in life to a post or a partnership in one of the Medici houses. A typical case is that of Gierozzo dei Pigli, who in 1446 was sent to take charge of the business in London. According to the terms of the contract, Cosimo dei Medici and Giovanni Benci supplied the bulk of the capital, Gierozzo contributing about a sixth. The senior partners took four-fifths of the profits, leaving one-fifth to their London manager. If the business should be run at a loss, "which God forbid", the losses would be shared in the same proportion. The young man had to promise not to dice or gamble, and was given detailed instructions as to the firms to whom he could safely lend, the amount of credit which he could give, the house in which to lodge and the company which he might keep. Gierozzo's name figures nine years later in a contract relating to the bank at Bruges. Here the senior partners are Piero, Giovanni and Pierfrancesco dei Medici, who contribute £1,900 of the total capital of £3,000 and take three-fifths of the profits. Gierozzo contributes £600, and Angelo Tani, who is to act as manager, £500; both receive a fifth of the profits.[1]

In 1465, Tommaso Portinari, brother of the manager of the bank at Milan, was put in charge at Bruges, and held office for fifteen years. His activities are a good example of the multifarious business transacted by the bank. He bought English wool, sometimes having it woven locally and sent to Florence for finishing. He sold Florentine silks and brocades to the Flemish nobility, and cotton, sugar and spices sent to him from the Venice house. He bought Gobelin tapestries and other works of art to furnish the Medici palace in Florence. He made it possible, by means of bills of exchange, for Campobasso

[1] The *libra de' grossi*, or pound, was equivalent to twelve Florentine gold florins.

and other Italian mercenaries in the service of Charles the Bold, Duke of Burgundy, to send their earnings home. He established confidential relations with the Duke, lending him money for his campaigns, and acting as Lorenzo's agent at the Burgundian court. In 1466 he built a fine new bank-house and sent a pressing invitation to Lorenzo to visit it.

Some of the branch managers were related to the Medici by marriage, such as the Tornabuoni brothers in Rome, and Leonetto Rossi, the husband of Lorenzo's eldest sister Maria, at Lyons. A post of special importance was that of manager of the home office in Florence; to this Francesco Sassetti succeeded shortly after Cosimo's death, and Lorenzo made him his chief adviser in business matters. In addition to the business of their banks, the Medici were also partners in firms connected with the silk and woollen industries in Florence. Lorenzo, who was by right of birth a member of the *Arte del Cambio*, was enrolled in the *Arte di Calimala* at the age of ten and in the *Arte di Seta* when he became head of the family. As a member of three of the greater guilds, he occupied a key position in Florentine commerce. The Medici were not without business rivals—conspicuous among them being the Pazzi who had independent banking establishments in Rome and Bruges—but in one way or another they were associated with almost all the great merchant families of Florence.

Lorenzo, in the opinion of his great-nephew, was not good at business. In all probability the Medici firm had outgrown one man's control, but he cannot escape from a share in the blame for the series of misfortunes which befell the business during his supremacy. There is evidence to show that the routine work suffered at his hands. Both Cosimo and Piero maintained close control over the management of the various branches. The correspondence relating to the Bruges house testifies, in particular to Piero's business sense, to the many letters which he wrote and the care with which he preserved them.

From 1470, the letters exchanged between Florence and Bruges became scarce. Lorenzo's dominant interests lay in politics and the arts rather than in banking, and he allowed too great licence to his subordinates, who in several instances abused their trust. Sassetti was sent a copy of the balance-sheet of all branches each year, but he grew careless in his review of the accounts, and failed to detect in time serious mismanagement of the Lyons branch by Leonetto de Rossi. Tommaso Portinari was no longer limited in the sums which he might lend from the Bruges bank on his own authority. He had a great admiration for Charles of Burgundy and lent money to him recklessly. Charles at his death left a huge unpaid debt to the bank, and Tommaso then threw good money after bad by lending to the Duke's son-in-law, Maximilian of Austria, whose impecuniosity was such that he was obliged to borrow from his bride to pay for the magnificent suit of silver armour in which he rode into Ghent for his wedding. In 1481, Lorenzo sold the Bruges bank to Portinari for the comparatively small sum of 16,616 florins.

Three years earlier, the London business was wound up under even less favourable conditions. Large sums lent to Edward IV during his struggle for the throne were not repaid. Warwick, too, borrowed from the bank, and the chances of recovery vanished with his fall. Gherardo Canigiani, the London manager, married an heiress, Dame Elizabeth Stockton, and became a naturalized Englishman. When Lorenzo sent Cristofano Spini to London to make a final settlement with regard to his interests, Canigiani repudiated the debts which he had incurred while acting on behalf of the Medici, and had Spini arrested. The bank in Florence was obliged to repay 51,533 florins borrowed from Bruges before the London business could be closed down. The crises in Bruges and London occurred at the time when Sixtus IV had quarrelled with Lorenzo and deprived the Medici of their position as papal bankers, as also of their monopoly of the

Tolfa alum mines. In 1478 Florence was plunged into war, and Lorenzo drew heavily on his own resources to meet the urgent need for money. All credits were drawn in by the Milanese bank, and Lorenzo even sold his share of the Medici villa at Cafaggiolo to his young cousins, the sons of Pierfrancesco. After the war, when the finances of Florence were overhauled and new taxes imposed, the special commission appointed to deal with the matter exempted Lorenzo from payment of the new taxes. They recognized that he was not in a position to pay, and that to expose the bad state of his finances would be to inflict grave injury to the city and government. Lorenzo was himself a member of the Commission, but constitutional procedure was duly observed, and it is explicitly recorded that he was not present when his private affairs were discussed and exemption from taxation granted to him.

Behind these temporary misfortunes and personal failures lay the general decline of Florentine trade in the latter part of the fifteenth century. Even before the discovery of the Cape route to the East and the consequent shifting of the trade paths, Italy, owing to foreign competition, was no longer the undisputed centre of European commerce. Growing nationalism exposed foreign merchants to the enmity of the natives. Florentine merchants could no longer ride about the Cotswolds buying all the wool they needed for the production of the heavy red cloth which was among their principal exports, as English weavers were making increasing demands on wool for their own cloth industry. Bans on imports made the search for new markets more difficult and bankers could not so easily find profitable ways of investing the money placed with them. A further disadvantage was the increase in the value of the gold florin, which diminished the profit made by the Medici bank on bills of exchange payable in this currency. Lorenzo inherited a tradition of lavish expenditure, which, in these less favourable conditions, was more than the business could bear. Yet the increasing importance of Florentine foreign relations called for more rather than less spending, and to cut down on charities and public works would have been to court unpopularity in the city. Thus throughout his ascendancy the vicissitudes of his business were among Lorenzo's chief anxieties.

A great commercial system, however, continues to function with some measure of prosperity long after it has passed its zenith. During Lorenzo's later years there are signs of revival in the Medici fortunes after the crisis through which they passed in the seventies. Under Innocent VIII Lorenzo once more enjoyed papal favour, and the Medici were reinstated in their old position of papal bankers. In 1483, Lorenzo was made Chamberlain of Naples, a post to which lucrative emoluments were attached. Owing to his revived friendship with King Ferrante, the Florentines became the most privileged community of foreign traders in Neapolitan territory. With the visit of Tommaso Portinari to Florence in 1489, friendly relations between himself and Lorenzo were re-established, and he, together with Cristofano Spini, was sent on an embassy to England which resulted in an important commercial treaty. On the one hand, England agreed that cargoes of wool carried on her ships should all be landed at Pisa and that none should be taken to Venice or Genoa. On the other hand, Florence promised that English ships alone should have the right of bringing wool to Pisa. Florence, in 1490, is another word for Lorenzo, and this famous treaty may be looked upon as the last important act in his career as a man of business.

Chapter Six

Ascendancy in Florence

(1469-78)

ACCORDING to an anonymous contemporary, the supremacy of the Medici in Florence rested upon three foundations. The first was a body of friends bound to them by common interests. The second was the support of the trade-guilds, which could be gained by seeing that all had their share of the honours of government and of the commercial advantages at the disposal of the state. The third was the favour of the populace, whose chief needs were security, food and entertainment. Later in life, in his drama *La Rappresentazione di San Giovanni e Paolo*, Lorenzo expressed the opinion that a ruler was worth little who could not make himself obeyed, especially in the early days of his supremacy. During the years which followed his rise to power all three foundations were maintained and strengthened, and his hold over Florence was made sure. One means of acquiring friends already practised by the Medici was that of marriage alliances with leading Florentine families. Tommaso Soderini, who had been instrumental in securing the invitation to Lorenzo to take the first place in the government, was married to a Tornabuoni and looked upon Lorenzo as a nephew. Marriages arranged for Piero's daughters brought the Rossi, the Pazzi and the Rucellai into the Medici circle. The last connexion was particularly valuable, as Bernardo Rucellai's father had been associated with Cosimo's opponents. From the time that he brought his bride home to the beautiful palace, built for the Rucellai by Leon Battista Alberti in the Via della

Nuova Vigna, his support for the Medici could be reckoned upon.

Lorenzo gave close attention both to the making of suitable marriages, and to preventing alliances which he considered politically undesirable. His sons-in-law included a Ridolfi and a Salviati, scions of rich and influential Florentine houses. He succeeded, moreover, in healing the rift between the two branches of the Medici family. A reconciliation with Pierfrancesco was effected at the time of Piero's funeral, and in order to seal the reunion, Lorenzo later betrothed his daughter Luigia to Pierfrancesco's younger son, Giovanni. Luigia's death at the age of eleven frustrated his intention, but during his own lifetime the family remained united. Only after his death did the quarrel break out afresh in a new and more dangerous form.

Other bonds besides that of matrimony added to Lorenzo's friends, and of these none is more important than that of common intellectual and artistic interests. It is characteristic of Medici generosity that scholars were allowed free access to their private library. A register was kept in which borrowers entered their names and those of the books which they took out. It is preserved today in the Florentine archives, and there, among many names which did not achieve fame, can be seen those of the leading men of letters of the age. A single page contains the signatures of Marsilio Ficino, Giovanni Lascaris and Angelo Poliziano. Ficino, the high-priest of neo-Platonism, was Lorenzo's guide in the realm of philosophy. Lascaris, a learned Greek, was employed to collect manuscripts from the East for the Medici library. Poliziano commended himself to Lorenzo by his translation of Homer. A poor boy from the little Tuscan town of Montepulciano, he was educated at Lorenzo's expense and became his greatest friend. As a poet he alone equalled, and indeed surpassed, his patron. Other intimates of the Medici were Matteo Franco, writer of sonnets, described by Lorenzo as one of the best-loved members of his household, and Luigi Pulci who entertained the company in the evenings by reading aloud the verses which were afterwards incorporated in his *Morgante*. Among the artists, Sandro Botticelli was proud to own himself the servant and protégé of the house of Medici, and Michelangelo owed his start in life as a sculptor to Lorenzo.

In the Laurentian age, the Medici circle was gay as well as learned. Cosimo was forty-five when he rose to power, and was treated with the deference due to his standing. Piero's ill-health cast a shadow over the society in which he moved. Now, for the first time, the leading citizen of Florence was a young man of immense vitality, as greedy for pleasure as he was for work. At his side was the best of companions, his brother Giuliano. In appearance he was tall and well-built, with sparkling eyes, an olive complexion and black hair. He was a fine athlete, delighting in hunting and dancing no less than in music, poetry and painting. He became the darling of Florence; even Machiavelli deigns to praise him as one in whom were united "all the beneficence and friendliness that could be desired in a man born to the highest fortune". There have been suggestions of rivalry between the brothers, but contemporary evidence bears out Poliziano's statement that they were devoted to one another. As he proclaimed in a Latin epigram, "Lorenzo, Giuliano—one spirit animates you both".

Giuliano had a romantic attachment to Simonetta, the wife of Marco Vespucci. Their loves provided a theme for poets, if they were not, as was long believed, immortalized in Botticelli's *Primavera*. It was said that in Florence a good joke attracted as much attention as a fine work of art, and both Lorenzo and Giuliano enjoyed joking. By their loves, their laughter, their songs and their sports they kept the city alive, as in their boyhood they had enlivened their country home at Cafaggiolo. The high-water mark of these brilliant days was the tournament of 1475, in which Giuliano played the leading part. The scene, as in Lorenzo's tournament, was the Piazza di Santa

Croce. On Giuliano's standard was a figure of Pallas in a golden tunic and bearing lance and shield, whilst Cupid was shown bound to the stump of an olive tree on a flowery meadow, with bow and broken arrows at his feet. Giuliano entered the lists wearing the favour of his lady-love and bore off the prize. The tournament is celebrated in Poliziano's *Stanze della Giostra di Giuliano dei Medici*. Unlike Pulci's *Giostra*, this lovely poem gives no minute description of the tournament. Its theme is Giuliano's resistance to the assaults of love, and love's final victory. When Giuliano issues in triumph from the combat, Simonetta appears to him, but is soon hidden in a thick cloud, an allusion to her sudden death in the following year. The *Stanze* are an idyll of Renaissance Florence, and a tribute to Lorenzo's achievements as its leader. They are dedicated to the "Laurel of happy birth, beneath whose shade Florence rests joyful and at peace".[1]

Among Lorenzo's earliest concerns was the introduction of reforms which would make the Florentine constitution a more effective instrument of government. Strong rule and continuity of policy could not easily be achieved by a chief magistracy which changed every two months, and the necessity of gaining the approval of three legislative councils before a measure initiated in the *Signoria* could become law caused intolerable delays in law-making. Yet both the multiplicity of councils and the bimonthly election of the *Signoria* were to the Florentines symbols of republican liberty and as such sacrosanct. All that Lorenzo could hope to do was to modify the existing system in such a way as to speed up legislation and to ensure that each *Signoria* which took office would be amenable to his will. Of recent years the magistrates had been chosen by a body of *accoppiatori* appointed for the purpose by the Council of a Hundred, and the Council had begun to show unwelcome independence by making alterations in the list presented to it by the dominant

[1] "Tu ben nato Laur' sotto il cui velo
Firenza lieta in pace si riposa."

faction. In 1470 it was proposed that the names of forty citizens who had acted as *accoppiatori* since 1434 should be put into a bag, together with five additional names, and that the *Signoria* should be selected by a committee of five, composed of names drawn annually from the bag. At once a cry was raised that the city was being delivered over to forty-five tyrants and the proposal was rejected.

A year later the same end was achieved by different means. The existing *Signoria* and *accoppiatori* appointed a *Balia*, which was enlarged by co-optation to a body of two hundred and forty members. Its duties were to hold a fresh scrutiny of those eligible for office, to select the magistrates for the next five years, and to reconstitute the Council of a Hundred in such a way as to give it authority to approve laws affecting the public interest without reference to the other councils. The changes were put into effect with the consent of a *Parlamento*, and were renewed in 1476 for another five years. Thus the Medici party was tolerably well assured of control over the government for some time to come. The complicated devices needed to secure even this small measure of centralization taught Lorenzo how carefully he must guard against any outward sign of despotic power. From letters addressed to him it is, however, clear that his voice was recognized to be the determining factor in the making of appointments. One citizen writes to reproach him for his exclusion from the *Balia*; another pleads that he has a large family and that it would be a great help to him if he were made *Gonfaloniere di Giustizia*. It was Lorenzo's daily task to deal with such requests so as to satisfy the petitioners as far as possible and at the same time to avoid letting any citizen become too powerful.

Another reform effected at the time was the strengthening of the ministry of justice (*Otto di Balia*) and the extension of its authority to the country districts. A police officer known as the *Bargello del Contado* was appointed with a mounted force to keep order and be on the look-out for signs of disaffection in the Florentine dominion. The government of her subject territory was always a weak spot in Florentine administration, as indeed it was in that of the majority of Italian city-states. Cities with a long tradition of independence resented being subject to a rival republic. The inhabitants of the country-side had no civic rights, and were looked upon by the Florentines chiefly as a source of food and revenue in the shape of tolls paid on the corn, wine and oil which they brought into the city.

An example of the danger to Florence arising from the chronic state of discontent outside her walls occurred at Prato shortly after Lorenzo's assumption of power. Bernardo Nardi, who had been involved in the Neroni conspiracy, swooped down upon Prato with a band of exiles, and managed to gain possession of the public palace, where they held the Florentine Podestà a prisoner. Bernardo harangued the citizens from the balcony, recalling their ancient liberties and bidding them rise against their oppressors. When his words produced no immediate response, he threatened to hang the Podestà from the palace windows, but the latter, Cesare Petrucci by name, with great promptitude and courage, asked and obtained leave to address the people himself, as one whom they were accustomed to obey. His action gave time for a young knight of Rhodes who happened to be in Prato to raise volunteers, and with their aid to overwhelm Nardi and his supporters. Thus a movement was crushed which might have led to a general rising in Tuscany; for this Nardi had already been paving the way by fomenting disaffection among the peasants. The Prato episode may have prompted the institution of the new police officer, but Lorenzo's chief method of dealing with the subject territory was not to use force but to make himself personally popular there. His success both in holding together and extending the Florentine dominion ranks among his most valuable achievements. The trouble which arose throughout the territory on the fall of the Medici is a testimony to the popularity of their rule.

Of all Tuscan cities subject to Florence, none resented her yoke so bitterly as Pisa. In the twelfth century, when Florence had not yet emancipated herself from the dominion of the Counts of Tuscany, Pisa ranked with Genoa and Venice as one of the great maritime republics of Italy. In conjunction with Genoa, she had driven the Saracens from Sardinia and established her own commercial supremacy in the island. Her ships took part in the first three Crusades and opened the path for her trade with the East. With the thirteenth century her decline set in. After her defeat by Genoa at the naval battle of Meloria (1284), her great days were over, and in 1406 a desperate struggle with Florence ended in her subjection. The Pisans continued to brood over their lost liberty, until Lorenzo turned their thoughts in a new direction by recalling to life their ancient university. By a regulation of 1472 Pisa was established as the principal university of the Florentine dominion. Lorenzo, as one of the directors, exerted himself to secure distinguished professors for his new foundation, and in due course sent his son Giovanni to study there in preparation for his ecclesiastical career. As has been noted in the previous chapter, he did his best to develop Pisa as a port, and he also bought large estates in the neighbourhood. Within the city the Medici owned a house with a garden running down to the Arno, and Lorenzo often stayed there with his family. Thus he established those personal relationships which were the surest means of winning the affections of the people. Under his auspices Pisa came as near to content as was possible for a city haunted by the memory of its past.

A more recent addition to the dominion was the Casentino. This lovely mountain valley, through which the infant Arno flows on its way towards Arezzo, was taken from the Count of Poppi, after the battle of Anghiari (1440), in which he had sided with the enemies of Florence. The Castle of Poppi now became the seat of a Florentine Podestà, and the arms of those who ruled there in the name of the Republic are still displayed on its walls. In the hills above was the monastery of Camaldoli, founded by San Romualdo, its abbot at this time being Mariotto Allegri, an enthusiastic Platonist and Lorenzo's friend. During the summer months, members of the Platonic Academy met there as guests of the abbot. Lorenzo and Giuliano dei Medici were among the scholarly company who sat under the shade of the great trees and philosophized to the accompaniment of a babbling mountain stream. Higher up, at the Eremo, a body of monks lived, each in his separate cell, meeting only to perform the *Opus Dei*, the daily round of offices which have been said there without intermission from the eleventh century until today.

Another close link between the Medici and the Casentino lay in Bibbiena, where the principal family of the little town—the Dovizi—provided them with devoted servants. Piero da Bibbiena, as he was commonly known, was Lorenzo's private secretary. His brother Bernardo was the tutor and later the secretary of Lorenzo's second son, Giovanni, the future Pope Leo X. Another of the Dovizi, Antonio, was frequently employed by Lorenzo on diplomatic missions. Their loyalty to their patrons stood the test of adversity. A rising in favour of the Medici after their expulsion from Florence had its centre in Bibbiena and the Dovizi among its instigators.

The Medici villas were of considerable political importance in drawing the country districts into the orbit of the city. To the peasants of the Mugello the Medici were local squires, the *padroni* whose presence at harvest or vintage brought good fortune, and whose doings they followed with pride and interest. Lorenzo realized the value of these centres of loyalty when he built his villas at Poggio a Caiano, on the road to Pistoia, and at Spedaletto, in the neighbourhood of Volterra. After his son Giovanni had received minor orders at the age of eight, a hunt for benefices began which served the double purpose of adding to the lands and revenues of the Medici and strengthening their influence at strategic points in Tuscany. Throughout the dominion the Medici came to be regarded as personal lords, whose rule was preferred by the cities to that of a rival republic, and who in many parts of the country-side were well liked because they were well known.

The story of the revolt of Volterra and its suppression is a miserable exception to Lorenzo's successful dealing with the Florentine dominion. The episode has cast a slur on his name which cannot be obliterated, and until this day the spirit of partisanship pervades every account of it.[1] Among the tangle of issues which complicate the history of the revolt, rivalry between factions in Volterra is at least as important as tension between Florence and a subject city, or Lorenzo's personal interest in the mining of alum. Volterra first placed itself under the protection of Florence in 1361; from that time it had a resident Florentine *Capitano* and paid an annual tribute, remaining in other respects a self-governing commune, with its elected magistrates and councils. In 1470 a private company, comprising three Florentines, three Sienese and two Volterrans, obtained a contract for mining alum in the territory, the concession being ratified by the General Council of Volterra. The legality of the contract was disputed on the ground that the decision of the Council had not been unanimous, and in June 1471 newly elected magistrates seized the mine, driving out the workmen and officials of the company. At this point Florence intervened and sent an emissary from the *Signoria* to reinstate the holders of the concession. Meeting with active resistance from members of the opposing faction, the latter relegated some of them to Florence. So far the quarrel had been mainly local. Inghirami and Riccobaldi, the two Volterrans in the company, were oligarchs, who

[1] Cf. Fiumi, E., *L'impresa di Lorenzo de' Medici contro Volterra* (1948). A full and authoritative enquiry into the facts, invariably placing on them the interpretation least favourable to Lorenzo.

looked to Florence and the Medici for support. It is possible that Inghirami's aim was to become lord of the city. Opposed to them were a number of citizens and peasants led by Francesco Cortugi, a champion of republican liberty and Inghirami's bitter enemy.

When the trouble began, Lorenzo wrote to the *Capitano* urging him to use tact and to be careful not to exasperate the Volterrans. Eventually the commune asked him to arbitrate in the dispute, and in February 1472 he gave his decision in favour of the company. Alum was an important factor in the production of Florentine cloth, and owing to the concession held by the Medici in the papal alum mines at Tolfa, they were personally interested in its supply. It was obviously to Lorenzo's advantage if the Volterran mine were in friendly hands, and although he was not himself a member of the company, he could count upon its co-operation. Among the Florentine members was Gino Capponi, scion of a family which was never subservient to the Medici. This and the invitation to Lorenzo to arbitrate suggest that although the company was friendly to him he did not control it. The Volterran authorities accepted his findings unreservedly. Apparently the original objection to the concession had been on the ground that too small a price had been paid for it. When, however, the company volunteered a larger sum, political passions had entered in and the offer was refused. Now the chief desire of the authorities was for a settlement which would put an end to civic strife. Hopes of peace were frustrated by the provocative behaviour of Inghirami and Riccobaldi, who took possession of the mine accompanied by an armed guard, and boasted loudly of their victory. Thereupon a popular rising broke out; Inghirami and his father-in-law took refuge in the house of the *Capitano*, whither they were pursued by the mob and killed. The *Capitano* promptly relegated certain members of the Inghirami faction to a safe distance from the city, and, having already removed the leaders of the opposing party, made strenuous efforts to restore peace and order.

At this point Lorenzo made the fatal decision to suppress the rising by force of arms. He was both angry and afraid. His friends had been assassinated, and Florentine exiles had invited the rebels to make common cause with them for the overthrow of the Medici. The Bishop of Volterra pleaded with him on behalf of many peaceful and well-disposed citizens, urging that order could be restored without recourse to arms, and cooler heads in Florence took the same view. Lorenzo, however, could not be moved from his purpose. He engaged Federico, Duke of Urbino, to bring 5,000 men to the attack, instructing him to finish the business as quickly as possible. The rebels on their side enlisted mercenaries and sought aid from the neighbouring states; they even offered to hand over Volterra to the King of Naples in return for his support. No power proved willing to give them effective help, and after less than a month they recognized that they must yield. Conditions of surrender were agreed upon which guaranteed the safety of the lives and property of the citizens. On hearing the news, Lorenzo wrote to the Florentine commissaries attached to the army, expressing his pleasure that Volterra had been recovered without suffering damage.

Before his letter reached them the city had been given over to plunder. How and when the sack started is by no means clear. According to the traditional story, mercenaries in the pay of Volterra admitted the Florentine troops into the city and joined with them in the loot. A clash between civic factions may have precipitated the outrage. The Duke of Urbino did nothing to restrain his men, and the luckless citizens were exposed to the full fury of the soldiery, suffering heavy loss of life and widespread destruction of property. Attempts have been made to suggest that Lorenzo was responsible for the sack, but, as he and all Florence realized, nothing could have been more fatal to his interests. Horror at the news put an end to joy in victory, and Lorenzo's deep concern is expressed in his exhortations to the Duke and the commissaries to do everything possible to localize the trouble, to call off the troops and punish the wrong-doers. Lorenzo was no more to blame for the disaster than was Charles V for the sack of Rome. The greed and violence of mercenaries and the inability of their commanders to enforce discipline were responsible alike for the major and the minor tragedy.

Although Lorenzo contributed generously to relief of suffering and repair of the damage, the harm done was irreparable. Volterra became a nest of malcontents, held down by a fortress built for the purpose. Many of the city's privileges were withdrawn and Florence assumed control of its territory. As to the alum mine over which the trouble began, it was taken over by the *Arte di Lana*, which deputed some of the original company to work it. Shortly afterwards mining stopped owing to technical difficulties. It began again when Sixtus IV's withdrawal of the Tolfa concession from the Medici caused a shortage of alum in Florence, but in 1483 it was finally abandoned, as the produce of the mine did not justify the expense of working. The pitifulness of the disaster is enhanced by the sense of how easily it might have been averted. At every point peaceful intentions had been overborne by the spirit of enmity and fear. Lorenzo was among those who at a critical moment allowed passion to triumph over reason. He was false to his principle that subject cities must be wooed and not coerced, and the consequences of his action earned for him the undying hatred of the people of Volterra.

Chapter Seven

Foreign Relations

(1469-78)

DURING the early years of Lorenzo's ascendancy, the foreign relations of Florence were no less favourable to him than her internal government. The two were closely connected, for, as the Ferrarese ambassador noted, Lorenzo's reputation in Florence was largely determined by the consideration shown for him by foreign powers. As always, the problem of foreign policy was how to keep the peace which all Italian rulers knew to be in their best interests, when each state had ambitions which conflicted with those of its neighbour. Romagna—well named the nervous system of Italy—was a perennial source of trouble. Its cities were ruled by local despots, among them the Malatesta of Rimini, the Manfredi of Imola and Faenza, the Ordelaffi of Forli, and the Sforza of Pesaro. Whilst they acknowledged papal suzerainty, they did their best to render suzerain authority ineffective. The fierce separatism of the citizens helped to keep the despots in power, yet the people suffered from the attempt to maintain a more sumptuous state than their revenues warranted, and there was an undercurrent of discontent which easily became rebellion. The Popes, on their side, had not sufficient forces at their command to bring the province under their direct rule, so they recognized the despots as Vicars of the Church in their respective cities, thus regularizing a situation which they could not prevent. Meanwhile they were on the look-out for opportunities of substituting their own rule for that of individual despots.

Neighbouring states were tempted by the chronic

unrest in Romagna to intervene for purposes of their own. Venice already held Ravenna and Cervia, the former being valuable to her for its port on the Adriatic and the latter for its salt-pans, and she hoped to acquire other cities. Both Florence and Milan sought to gain influence in Romagna by taking some of the local despots under their protection. Faenza, commanding the Val Lamone, facilitated Florentine trade with the East by securing easy access to the Adriatic, and the Manfredi gladly accepted Florence as their patron. Francesco Sforza founded an allied dynasty in Pesaro by buying the city for his brother. Sforza and Medici alike came to regard the maintenance of the power of the Bentivoglio in Bologna as a matter of major importance in preserving the independence of the city and its neighbours. When, after the assassination of Annibale Bentivoglio in 1446, there was no member of the family of an age to succeed to his position, Cosimo encouraged Sante, a cousin of the murdered man, to leave his work as a wool merchant in Florence and accept the invitation of the Bolognese to become first citizen of the Republic. Sante's successful rule owed much to Cosimo's support, and not less to that of Francesco Sforza, who married him to his niece, Ginerva Sforza of Pesaro. On Sante's death, Giovanni, son of Annibale, succeeded both to his authority in Bologna and to his wife. In 1467, in order that he might have an armed force at his command, Florence, Milan and Naples took him into their joint service, each contributing 1,000 ducats a year towards his *condotta*. Allied intervention in Romagna on the part of the three powers did not please either the Pope or Venice, but it undoubtedly contributed to the cause of peace. The conclusion of the affair of Rimini, which in the summer of 1469 had threatened to cause a general conflagration, showed what could be achieved by Florence, Milan and Naples acting together.

When Lorenzo took up the threads of policy after his father's death, fighting had ceased in Rimini and Roberto Malatesta was in possession of the city. A year of strenuous diplomatic activity followed until at last, in December 1470, Paul II recognized Roberto as his Vicar and a general Italian peace was proclaimed. The most interesting feature of the negotiations is the claim of Florence, Milan and Naples that their alliance had the same object as the Italian League of 1455, namely the peace of Italy. It was put forward by them in a formal renewal of their treaty of friendship, as also in their diplomatic correspondence. All three made their own contribution to the common cause. Lorenzo instructed his envoy to plead with the Pope for the recognition of Roberto on the ground that it would remove a cause of quarrel and pave the way for the renewal of the League. Naples urged Milan to sink her differences with Venice for the sake of unity. The Duke of Milan assured the Pope of the great importance attached by the Triple Alliance to a peace which would include all the Italian powers, Rimini among them. Fortune, in the shape of the capture of Negropont by the Turks, played into their hands. Venice now urgently desired peace at home, and all the powers realized the need for presenting a united front to the growing Turkish menace. Thus Paul II was able to bring about a renewal of the League of 1455. When the danger lessened, rivalries between the Italian states came to the fore and the pact was again broken. All were sincere in their belief in the League as the surest means by which peace could be preserved, but each state adhered to it with the reservation saving its own interests. Lorenzo's first year's experience of diplomacy determined the lines of his future policy. His aim was always Italian peace. For its preservation he looked to the Triple Alliance acting on the principles of the League. He saw that attempts on the independence of the smaller states, especially on those of Romagna, would lead to general war, and constituted himself their champion and guardian.

The relations between Florence, Milan and Naples were never more friendly than in the years which followed the renewal of the League. In 1471 the Duke and Duchess of Milan paid an eight-day visit to Florence. The ducal retinue numbered some two thousand persons; nobles and courtiers were clad in cloth of gold and silver, and the servants wore new suits of silk. With the company came dogs, falcons and hawks, in order that the journey might be enlivened by hunting. Never had the Florentines seen such pomp. They, like other republicans, took peculiar interest in the doings of princes and, although there was some grumbling over the expense of entertaining so large a suite, the distinguished visitors gave general pleasure. Galeazzo and his Duchess were the guests of the Medici, and with them came the Duke's illegitimate daughter Caterina, a child of about eight. Her future relations with the Medici were not always happy, but she never forgot her first visit to Florence, where the beauty of the city and the treasures of the palace in the Via Larga made a deep impression on her. Here the sight of paintings, sculptures, jewels, vases, chosen and arranged with exquisite taste, caused the Duke to remark that however great the sum expended money alone could never produce a collection to rival that of his hosts. Florentine talent showed itself in songs in praise of the Milanese as they entered the city, and in sacred dramas acted in different churches on three successive days. During the performance of the descent of the Holy Spirit at Santo Spirito, a fire broke out which did great damage to the church built some years earlier by Brunelleschi. The Florentines saw in the disaster a sign of divine displeasure at the profanity of the Milanese, who, although it was Lent, ate meat every day of their visit. A permanent memorial of the occasion was the fine portrait of the Duke painted by Antonio Pollaiuolo, which for long hung in the Medici palace and is now in the Uffizi.

Later in the year Paul II died, and Francesco della Rovere became Pope Sixtus IV. Lorenzo headed the Florentine embassy of congratulation to the new pontiff, and was received with the greatest cordiality. The Medici were confirmed in their office of bankers to the Papacy, whilst the concessions granted them in the Tolfa alum mines were renewed and amplified. Lorenzo was allowed to buy gems and cameos from Paul II's collection at a moderate price. He also received two marble busts as a personal present from the Pope. Soon afterwards, Sixtus IV's nephew, Pietro Riario, was made Archbishop of Florence; friendly relations between Lorenzo and the Papacy seemed assured. Before his election, Sixtus had been General of the Franciscans, but his life had little in common with that of his patron. His chief interests were the advancement of his numerous Riario and della Rovere nephews and the patronage of the arts.

Typical of the extravagant, half-pagan atmosphere of the Curia during his reign was the sumptuous banquet given by Cardinal Pietro Riario to Leonora of Aragon when she passed through Rome on her way to Ferrara as the bride of Duke Ercole d'Este. Scenes from classical mythology were reproduced in confectionery, and a poem written for the occasion told how the gods failed to obey Jove's summons to a council because they were busy serving at the cardinal's table. Leonora's wedding journey is one of the triumphal progresses of the Renaissance, and nowhere was she received with greater honour than in Florence. Her stay in the city coincided with the feast of St. John Baptist, the hey-day of the Florentine year. On her arrival, seven scenes representing the mysteries of the Christian faith were performed for her entertainment. On St. John's Eve she watched the customary procession of the guilds, headed by the *Signoria*, who went to lay their gifts upon the altar at the Baptistery. Next day the annual race for the *Palio* took place, when horses and riders forged their way through the crowded streets, and all Florence was noisy and happy. In the evening, the *Signoria* gave a banquet at which Lorenzo and Giuliano waited upon the chief guest. All these doings were described by Leonora in a letter to a friend, and they drew from King Ferrante a warm expression of gratitude to Lorenzo. The pleasure given to his daughter had, he said, increased his affection for him, if indeed increase were possible. Not long afterwards, Florence welcomed a visitor of a more sober kind. Christian I of Denmark came there primarily to see a Greek manuscript of the Gospels recently brought from Constantinople. He declined all ceremonies, and his modest retinue contrasted with the splendours of the Milanese and the Neapolitans. The wiser heads in Florence commented with approval on his dignity and simplicity.

A source of great satisfaction to Lorenzo were the signs of confidence shown to him by Louis XI of France. After the withdrawal of René of Anjou from Italy in 1464 had sealed his failure to win the throne of Naples, Louis adopted a new policy towards the Italian states. He ceased to press the claims of French princes to Naples and Milan, and set himself to increase his own influence south of the Alps by cultivating the friendship of the leading powers. Now the Duke of Milan was holding Genoa as a fief of France, and was married to the King's sister-in-law, whilst the Medici had been given the right to bear the royal arms. In 1473 Louis wrote to Lorenzo asking for his help in opening negotiations with King Ferrante for a marriage between the Dauphin and a Neapolitan princess, a step towards reconciliation between rival claimants to the throne which proved abortive. He also suggested that Lorenzo should send a confidential agent to the French court. Such an agent would provide them with a useful channel of communication, but he must be warned against intimacy with the princes of the blood who were the king's natural enemies. The letter ended with a request for a fine big dog to be the writer's companion and protector.

The honeymoon period of Lorenzo's relations with Sixtus IV proved to be of short duration. Within a few years the erstwhile friends had become implacable enemies. Sixtus practised nepotism on an unprecedented scale; no fewer than six of his clerical nephews were made cardinals, and his aim was to provide for the laymen of his family by making them lords of cities in the states of the Church. Trouble began over the little town of Imola, which was sold by Taddeo Manfredi to the Duke of Milan. Lorenzo considered that Imola, no less than the other Manfredi city of Faenza, lay within his sphere of influence. He was already negotiating for its purchase by Florence when Sixtus intervened and bought it for Girolamo Riario, providing at the same time for his marriage with Caterina Sforza. Thereupon Lorenzo put difficulties in the way of raising the 40,000 ducats which Sixtus required for the purchase, and the latter retaliated by transferring his account from the Medici bank to that of the rival firm of Pazzi. Another cause of quarrel arose when Sixtus sent a force to eject Niccolò Vitelli from the lordship of Città di Castello. The town lay in the Tiber valley close to the Florentine border, and the threat to its independence at once brought Lorenzo to Vitelli's aid. Although he could not prevent his overthrow he gave him shelter in Florentine territory, where he awaited the opportunity to return to power.

Meanwhile Sixtus pursued his purpose by making another nephew, Giovanni della Rovere, Papal Vicar of Sinigaglia and prefect of Rome. He further arranged for his marriage with the eldest daughter of the Duke of Urbino, an alliance which in the next generation added Urbino to the della Rovere possessions. There was now rapidly increasing antagonism between Lorenzo and the Pope. The former opposed by every means in his power the attempt to make Riario and della Rovere dominant in the states of the Church, and continued to act as the champion of the native lords. Sixtus had gone out of his way to show favour to Lorenzo, even to the extent of sending him help against Volterra. In return he expected co-operation from him, and found him instead the chief obstacle in his path. The sudden death of Pietro Riario in 1474 extended the quarrel to the ecclesiastical sphere.

The Pope proposed to make Francesco Salviati Riario's successor as Archbishop of Florence, but yielded to Lorenzo's request that his brother-in-law Rinaldo Orsino should be appointed. When he nominated Salviati to the Archbishopric of Pisa by way of compensation, the Florentine government flatly refused to give him possession of the see. The reasons for Lorenzo's objections to Salviati are obscure, but he looked on the appointment as a violation of an undertaking that sees in Florentine territory should not be filled without the consent of the *Signoria*. Sixtus was indignant at the high-handed action which kept his nominee out of his archbishopric, and the breach between Florence and Rome widened.

In north Italy relations between Milan and Venice continued to be hostile, each aspiring to extend their frontier at the other's expense. It thus appeared to be a worthy contribution to the cause of peace when, through Lorenzo's efforts, a league between Florence, Milan and Venice was formed, provision being made for the Pope and Naples to enter it if they consented. Far from contributing to general peace, the league prompted a counter-league between Rome and Naples. Sixtus protested that the object of the alliance was his isolation, and Ferrante was offended at a step taken by his friends without consulting him, all the more as he regarded Venice as a serious rival to Naples in the Adriatic. Friendly relations between Florence and Naples continued for the time being, but there was no longer the same harmony as before. Four years after the Italian league had been renewed, the major powers were divided into two mutually suspicious groups.

During the Christmas festival of 1476, the Duke of Milan was assassinated by three young citizens as he was about to enter the Church of Santo Stefano. Galeazzo Maria Sforza inherited many of the more unpleasant characteristics of his Visconti ancestors. He was cruel, licentious and vindictive, and in contrast to his soldier father, militarily undistinguished. Nevertheless he was a capable ruler and by no means unpopular with his subjects. His assassins, inspired by ideal love of liberty, trusted that the citizens would seize the opportunity to throw off a tyrant's yoke, but the first thought of the Milanese was to avenge their prince's murder. His son, the seven-year-old Gian Galeazzo, whose christening Lorenzo had attended, was at once proclaimed Duke, under the guardianship of his mother. Sixtus IV said on hearing the news "the peace of Italy is dead", and no one realized the truth of his words more fully than Lorenzo. Galeazzo Maria had been his steady friend, believing wholeheartedly in the need for Florence and Milan to work together. For the next few years the government of Milan was weakened by the feud between the Duchess and her Chancellor on the one hand and the Duke's uncles on the other, and could not be relied upon for support in Italian politics. Not long ago all the powers of Italy appeared to be Lorenzo's friends. Now, as he approached the supreme crisis of his life, he stood practically alone.

Chapter Eight

The Pazzi Conspiracy

VITTORIO ALFIERI'S *La Congiura dei Pazzi,* written in 1776, is inspired by the author's passionate desire to see Italy freed from the yoke of the foreigner, a united and independent nation. The Pazzi, as he portrays them, have similar aspirations, and their aim is to free Florence from a tyrant. Those responsible for the tragic events which took place in Florence in 1478 were actuated by less noble motives; they raised the cry of liberty, but they did so in pursuit of private enmities and personal ambitions. The Pazzi were an old and proud family who had made for themselves a name in Florentine history long before there is any mention of the Medici. A Pazzi returned from the First Crusade bringing with him fire from the altar of the Holy Sepulchre at Jerusalem. His descendants became guardians of the ancient flints from which each year the new fire is kindled in the Cathedral of Florence, and his exploit is still commemorated in the ceremony known as the *Scoppio del Carro.* On Easter Eve the chariot of the Pazzi is drawn by milk-white oxen to the Piazza del Duomo, and a mechanical dove flies out of the west door to light the fireworks with which the *carro* is decorated.

Cosimo dei Medici freed the Pazzi from the disabilities imposed on the nobility, thus enabling them to take their full share in trade and politics. A witness to their prosperity in the fifteenth century is the beautiful Pazzi chapel adjoining the Church of Santa Croce built for them by Brunelleschi. As bankers they were independent, and to some extent rivals, of the Medici, but they were brought together by the marriage of Guglielmo dei Pazzi to

Lorenzo's sister Bianca, and relations between the two families remained friendly until Sixtus IV applied to the Pazzi for the purchase money he needed to acquire Imola. Lorenzo asked them to refuse, but they ignored his request and provided the sum which enabled Girolamo Riario to become lord of the city. This was tantamount to a declaration of war, and from that time Francesco dei Pazzi, the manager of the Roman bank, was the prime mover in the plot which aimed at the overthrow of the Medici and the elevation of the Pazzi to the first place in Florence. Closely associated with him was Girolamo Riario, bent on increasing his possessions in Romagna, and convinced that the elimination of Lorenzo would remove the chief obstacle to his mastery of the whole province. A third malcontent was Francesco Salviati, who had spent the greater part of the last three years in Rome waiting in vain to gain possession of the Archbishopric of Pisa which the Florentines withheld from him. While these three worked out the preliminaries of the plot, the Pazzi in Florence found fresh cause for hating the Medici. One of the family had married the daughter and heiress of Giovanni Borromeo, and expected to succeed to her fortune. His hopes were frustrated by the passing of a law which enabled the dead man's nephews to establish their claim to inherit in the daughter's place. The Pazzi traced Lorenzo's hand in a piece of legislation which served the double object of punishing them for their disobedience over Imola, and benefiting the Borromei who were staunch Mediceans.

For all this, Francesco dei Pazzi had difficulty in persuading his relatives in Florence to take part in an attempt to overthrow the Medici by force. Jacopo, the head of the family, notorious gambler though he was, considered the risk too great, and when he was first approached on the subject was "colder than ice". In the end Francesco succeeded in inducing him and other members of the family to fall in with the plans being made in Rome. Renato dei Pazzi, however, held aloof from the plot; he had no love for the Medici, but he suggested that as Lorenzo was hard pressed for money, a safer way to ruin him would be to lend to him at high interest. As far as can be ascertained, Lorenzo's brother-in-law, Guglielmo, was kept in ignorance of the whole affair.

The conspirators realized that their success depended on the murder of both the Medici brothers. To kill Lorenzo and to leave the much-loved Giuliano alive would be to court disaster. A mercenary captain in Riario's service, Gian Battista da Montesecco by name, was cast for the rôle of assassin, and when the deed was done Jacopo dei Pazzi was to rouse the city to revolt in the name of liberty. Meanwhile troops from Imola, and a force from Città di Castello, under Lorenzo Giustini, the successful rival of the Vitelli, were to hold themselves in readiness for an invasion of Florentine territory in order to assist in effecting a change of government. Montesecco from the first was reluctant to play the part assigned to him, and he insisted that he would not undertake it until he had heard from the Pope's own lips that he sanctioned what was proposed. Thus the conspirators found it necessary to lay their plans before Sixtus IV, Montesecco being present at the interview. The deposition which he made after his arrest is the authority for the discussion which took place in the Vatican. "I wish the government to be taken out of Lorenzo's hand," said Sixtus; "he is a violent and bad man who pays no regard to us. If he were expelled, we could do as we willed with the Republic." Although he agreed to the use of force in order to overthrow the government of Florence, he refused to countenance murder. Montesecco pointed out to him that unless Lorenzo and Giuliano were killed, it was unlikely that their object could be achieved, but he reiterated that he would have no one die. Salviati, however, assured him that the bark of their enterprise should be steered safely into harbour, and ultimately he expressed himself as content. Assassination was no novelty in Renaissance Italy, and Sixtus could hardly fail to be aware of the probable course of events. The conclusion which the conspirators drew from the interview was that the Pope desired the end in view too much to be over particular as to the means. They departed, promising him that once Florence was in his hands he could dictate to half Italy.

The next problem was to seek out an occasion for committing the crime. At first it was proposed to lure Lorenzo to Rome on a visit from which, said Riario, he would not return, provision being made to dispose of Giuliano elsewhere. Lorenzo, however, declined the invitation, and the conspirators gathered in Florence to await an opportunity of killing both brothers together. Here Rafaello Riario, a youth of sixteen who was studying at the University of Pisa and had lately been made a cardinal, became the innocent tool of his uncle Girolamo. He was invited to stay with Jacopo dei Pazzi in his villa outside Florence, and instructed to write a friendly letter to Lorenzo, in response to which he was asked to visit the Medici villa at Fiesole. Once more the plans of the conspirators went awry as Giuliano was ill and did not accompany his brother to meet his guest. Rafaello next expressed a wish to see the treasures of the Medici palace, and it was arranged that he should come into Florence on the following Sunday, and, after being present at High Mass in the Cathedral, dine in the Via Larga. The assassins were to do their work during the meal, but at the last moment it was learned that Giuliano was not well enough to take part in the banquet, although he intended to be at Mass. Thus it was agreed that the murder must take place during the service in the Cathedral. At this point Montesecco declined to act. Since the plot was first mooted he had been sent by Riario on a mission to Lorenzo and had fallen under his spell. The meeting took place at Cafaggiolo, and Lorenzo's friendly conversation, as the two rode into Florence together afterwards, increased Montesecco's dislike of the task assigned to him. Now the change of plan gave him fresh cause to object, and he flatly refused to commit a murder at Mass "where

God would see him". In his place two priests undertook the responsibility of killing Lorenzo; one had been Jacopo dei Pazzi's secretary, and the other, as a native of Volterra, was eager to avenge his city's wrongs. Francesco dei Pazzi and Bernardo Bandini Baroncelli, a member of a family associated with the Pazzi in business who had himself fallen on evil days, were chosen as Giuliano's murderers.

When the company assembled in the Cathedral on the fatal April 26, it was noticed that Giuliano had not arrived. His assassins went to look for him, and on meeting him, Pazzi put his arm round him in an apparently friendly gesture, which enabled him to make sure that his victim was not wearing mail. The prearranged signal for the attack was the ringing of the sanctuary bell, but contemporary accounts are not agreed on the precise point in the service; some say at the elevation of the Host, some at the *Agnus Dei*, some not until the *Ite Missa est*. When the moment came, Baroncelli instantly plunged his dagger into Giuliano's side, causing him to reel against Francesco dei Pazzi. The latter followed up the attack with great ferocity until Giuliano lay dead on the pavement, his body pierced by nineteen wounds. Lorenzo was outside the choir on the south side of the altar when the two priests attacked him. They, however, were less expert at their work, and by drawing his sword and wrapping his cloak over his left arm as a shield, he was able to parry their blows. Jumping over the light railing which enclosed the choir at this period, he ran in front of the altar pursued by his brother's murderers until he reached safety in the north sacristy. His friends shut the heavy bronze doors behind him, and one of them sucked the wound in his neck lest the dagger which had struck him should have been poisoned. Because Lorenzo lived, the Pazzi conspiracy had failed.

Within the Cathedral confusion reigned. Some people fled to their homes, some went into hiding, some returned bearing arms in Lorenzo's defence, others waited to see how the situation would develop. Cardinal Rafaello remained terrified and alone by the altar, until some priests conducted him into the south sacristy, whither in course of time a guard was sent to arrest him. Archbishop Salviati had left the Cathedral earlier, and taking with him a body of men attempted to gain possession of the Palazzo Pubblico. He surprised the members of the *Signoria* at their Sunday dinner, but the *Gonfaloniere di Giustizia*—Cesare Petrucci—acted with the same promptitude and courage that he had shown as Podestà of Prato a few years before. He ordered the great bell to be rung, and with the aid of a chain drawn across the staircase kept the assailants at bay until the people flocked to the defence of the government. There was a moment of suspense in the city when a rumour spread that both the Medici had been killed, but once it was known that Lorenzo was alive and when he appeared with his bandaged neck on the balcony of his own house, the mass of the people rallied round him. Jacopo dei Pazzi, riding through the streets crying *Popolo e Libertà*, was greeted with curses and shouts of *Palle, Palle*. Florence proceeded to take such vengeance on the traitors as in Guicciardini's words, "passed all civilized bounds". Francesco dei Pazzi and Archbishop Salviati, with two members of his family, were hung out of hand from the windows of the Palazzo Pubblico. Jacopo dei Pazzi and the two priests were ferreted out of their hiding-places some days later to share the same fate; Jacopo having first been tortured and the two priests mutilated. Renato dei Pazzi was also hung, as an accessory before the fact. Baroncelli escaped into Turkish territory, but was handed over by the Sultan at Lorenzo's request and brought back to Florence to die in the following year. Montesecco, after writing a full confession of his share in the conspiracy, was given a soldier's death by the sword. In all some eighty persons were killed, many of them innocent victims of mob violence.

If savagery and brutality were characteristic of the

times, no less typical was the spirit which brought the arts into play to commemorate the fate of traitors. The principal conspirators were portrayed in fresco on the walls of the prison adjoining the Palazzo Pubblico by Sandro Botticelli, to whom the Republic paid forty florins for his work. They were represented hanging by the neck owing to the manner of their death, except for Napoleone Francesi, who made his escape and was painted hanging by the foot, as an exile. Lorenzo himself composed the descriptive verses which figured under each portrait. Here they remained for all to see until the frescoes were destroyed on the expulsion of the Medici in 1494. Giuliano was buried on Ascension Day, a feast associated by the Florentines with going out into the fields to greet the spring and catch grasshoppers. This year it became a day of mourning, and crowds flocked to San Lorenzo to pay their last tribute to one who had contributed much to the gaiety of Florentine life. It was discovered that he had left an illegitimate son who had been christened Giulio. Lorenzo at once took the child into his household, and had him trained for an ecclesiastical career, thus setting his feet on the path which culminated in his accession to the Papacy as Clement VII.

The attempt of the Pazzi to destroy the power of the Medici had in fact increased Lorenzo's hold on Florence. It had been made plain that no class in the city—neither the merchants, the shop-keepers nor the populace—favoured the substitution of a Pazzi for a Medici ascendancy. The action of two of the Cavalcanti, who when Lorenzo was flying before his pursuers in the Cathedral protected him with their swords, showed that even the old noble families to which the Pazzi belonged were not unanimous in supporting them. By their ill-judged bid for power they had compassed their own ruin. Some members of the family were imprisoned, and all were disgraced. Lorenzo's own brother-in-law, Guglielmo, who had accompanied him on his first diplomatic mission, was confined for a time to his villa outside Florence.

Within the city Lorenzo's popularity was never greater, but he had yet to reckon with external enemies. Girolamo Riario was eagerly awaiting news from Florence; when he learned of the failure of the plot and its consequences, his anger knew no bounds. His troops seized the person of the Florentine ambassador, Donato Acciaiuoli, who was only saved from imprisonment by the protests of the Venetian and Milanese representatives against this violation of diplomatic immunity. Sixtus IV, egged on by his nephew, issued a Bull of Excommunication against "that son of iniquity and child of perdition" Lorenzo dei Medici, in which he set out at length all his causes of complaint against him, beginning with his championship of Niccolò Vitelli and other enemies of the Church, and culminating in the execution of Archbishop Salviati and the arrest and imprisonment of Cardinal Rafaello Riario. The *Gonfaloniere* and *Priori* of Florence were included in the excommunication, and an interdict was pronounced upon the entire city and territory unless the offenders were brought to punishment within a month. As Lorenzo wrote to Louis XI of France in reply to his warm letter of condolence, his real crime in the Pope's eyes was that he had not let himself be killed. Nevertheless, the hanging of an archbishop without trial, the imprisonment of a cardinal and the assassination of several members of his suite by the mob, provided ample reason for ecclesiastical censures, and the attitude of defiance assumed by the Florentine government heightened its offence. On the urgent advice of Acciaiuoli from Rome, Rafaello Riario was set at liberty, but the interdict was treated as of no effect and the clergy were ordered to perform their functions as usual. St. John Baptist Day was observed that year, a week late it is true, but with all its customary festivities.

Excommunication and interdict were followed by a declaration of war against Florence, not only by the Papacy but by Naples. There was, as has been noted, already a rift between Florence and the Neapolitan government. Now Sixtus IV's determination to take arms lured Ferrante, and more particularly his ambitious son Alfonso, into the temptation of employing their undoubted military superiority to make the House of Aragon the dominant power in Tuscany. For Florence the situation was perilous in the extreme. The city was quite unprepared for war, and early in July Neapolitan forces were within Florentine territory. As always, when the liberties of the Republic were at stake, the citizens rose to the occasion. On the receipt of a letter from the Pope saying that Florence had only to expel Lorenzo to be restored to favour, the latter determined to appeal to the judgment of the people. A meeting of leading Florentines was summoned to the Palazzo, where a highly emotional scene took place. The events, said Lorenzo, which had killed his brother and threatened his own life had taught him that he had more enemies than he realized, but also more devoted friends. He, the Pope had declared, was the sole cause of the enmity shown by the Church to Florence, and it was for the Florentines to decide how best to act. For his own part, he placed himself unreservedly in their hands, and would gladly suffer exile or death if this would best serve the good of the Republic. He concluded by saying that, in order that he might devote himself more freely to the defence of the Republic, he had sent his wife and children to a place of safety outside the city, although, if need be, he would sacrifice even those dearest to him to the common cause. In reply, Jacopo dei Alessandri spoke in the name of those present, saying that all knew how much they owed to Lorenzo and were unanimous in their determination to stand by him. As a sign of how greatly he was loved and valued, and in view of the perils to which he was exposed, a guard of twelve men was appointed for his protection. A few days later the *Signoria* set up the customary committee known as the Ten of War to take charge of the coming campaign, Lorenzo being among its members. The city then threw itself into the work of preparing for battle.

Considerable encouragement was derived from the letters of sympathy and offers of help which poured in upon Lorenzo from many quarters. Immediately on the receipt of the news of the outrage in the Cathedral, Milan sent orders to Giovanni Bentivoglio to go to the defence of the Medici "*subito, subito, subito*". He had started across the Apennines even before the message reached him. During the war, Bologna provided passage for allied forces coming to the aid of Florence and winter-quarters for their troops. Although the papal legate, the nominal head of the Bolognese government, issued proclamations against harbouring the enemies of the Church, he found it politic to turn a blind eye on what was going on. Despite papal protests, both Milan and Venice sent aid to Florence, the Milanese contingent being led by Gian Giacomo Trivulzio, who was then at the beginning of his long and distinguished military career. Louis XI protested to the Pope against the attack made upon "our dear friend Lorenzo dei Medici", and followed up his protest by sending Philippe de Commynes as a special envoy to Rome. Every diplomatic weapon at his command was brought into play. There were threats of a General Council, hints of a revival of the Angevin claims to Naples and an *ordonnance* forbidding the remittance of money to Rome. But Sixtus remained obdurate and Louis set his face against armed intervention. Commynes, who spent nearly a year in Florence at this time, recorded in his *Mémoires* his regret at not being able to bring an army to aid the Florentines; he recognized that "le faveur du roi leur fit quelque chose mais non pas tant que j'eusse voulu". Fighting men were in fact Florence's chief need. Allied contingents were small and slow in coming, and her most effective forces were those of Niccolò, Count of Pitigliano, and other of Lorenzo's Orsini relations who entered Florentine service as *condottieri*.

It was not until the end of September that the Duke of Ferrara consented to begin operations as the commander-in-chief of the allied armies, and he, owing to his

Aragonese connexion, was at best a half-hearted champion. By this time Alfonso of Calabria and his Neapolitans were pressing up the Chiana valley, south of Florence, supported by papal forces under Federico, Duke of Urbino, who had a lifetime of military experience behind him. Siena, the age-long rival of Florence, provided a convenient base for the attack. Despite the advantages of the enemy, the campaign of 1478 ended inconclusively. Both sides adhered to the *condottiere* principle of avoiding pitched battles. Moreover, as modern soldiers have learned to their cost, the terrain of Central Italy with ranges of hills intersected by narrow valleys, and rivers which only impede transport, is not conducive to quick results. When the combatants retired into winter-quarters in November, the enemy was approaching the Arno valley, but was still a long way from Florence. During the 1479 campaign changes in the political situation worked unfavourably for the Florentines. The uncles of the young Duke of Milan, after being exiled by the Regent, had found asylum in Naples. Now, Ferrante, who had failed in his efforts to detach Milan from Florence, used the exiled Sforza brothers to secure his end. They appeared in the Lunigiana with the double purpose of furthering their own ambitions by an attack on the Milanese government and of weakening Ferrante's adversaries. Thereupon, the Milanese contingent fighting for Florence was recalled to the defence of its home territory, and with it went the Duke of Ferrara. In September, Lodovico Sforza was reconciled with the Duchess; the government, headed by the Chancellor Simonetta, fell and Lodovico became the effective ruler of Milan. On the very day of his *coup d'état* Neapolitan troops, operating in the Elsa valley, stormed the important fortress of Poggio Imperiale. No serious obstacle now lay between Alfonso and Florence, and with plague raging in the city, the country-side ravaged by war, the Republic stood little chance of resisting him. Alfonso, however, did not march on Florence, but pursued the less heroic course of mopping up small fortresses in the Val d'Elsa. A spirited resistance put up by the little town of Colle delayed him for two months, and on its fall he offered a truce, which Florence was thankful to accept.

Throughout the war Lorenzo remained in Florence engaged upon the task of keeping up supplies of men and money. Fresh taxes must continually be imposed in the form least calculated to arouse discontent, quarrelling *condottieri* must be kept apart, and allies pressed for increased aid. In addition, he was responsible for the conduct of a diplomatic war, waged on both sides with at least equal persistency to that which marked the war in the field. In the autumn of 1479 it became clear to him that Florence could not face another campaign. The resources of the Republic were strained to the uttermost, and to ask the citizens to make further sacrifices on his behalf would be to imperil his own position. He was also aware of a general desire for peace among the powers of Italy and of Europe. Such were the considerations which determined him to make a supreme effort to end the crisis and to go in person to Naples to win peace from King Ferrante. He left Florence secretly, and on December 7, from the Tuscan city of San Miniato Tedesco, addressed the following letter to the *Signoria*.

"Most illustrious Lords. If I did not inform you of the cause of my departure before I left Florence it was not from lack of respect, but because I held that the dangerous circumstances in which our city is placed demand action rather than deliberation. Peace it seems to me has become indispensable to us, and as all other means of obtaining it have proved fruitless, I have chosen to expose myself to some degree of danger rather than to allow the city to suffer longer under its present trials. Therefore, with your permission, I propose to go directly to Naples. As I am the person against whom the attack of our enemies is chiefly directed, I may by delivering myself into their hands, be the means of restoring peace to my fellow-citizens. One of two things is certain. Either the King of Naples is friendly to us, as he has often stated and as some have believed, and is attempting in his attack to serve us rather than to rob us of our liberties, or he desires the ruin of the Republic. If his intentions are good there is no better way of putting them to the test than by placing myself unreservedly in his hands; this I venture to say is the only way of obtaining an honourable peace. If, on the other hand, the King's aim is the destruction of our liberties, it is best to know the worst at once, and to learn at the expense of one rather than of many. I am glad to be that one, firstly because I being the principal object of hatred can more easily discover whether our enemies seek only to ruin me. Secondly, as I have had more honour and responsibility among you than my merits could claim, probably more than any private citizen has had in our day, I am more bound than any other person to serve my country, even at the risk of my life. With this intention I now go. Perhaps God wills that this war, which began in the blood of my brother and of myself, should be ended by my means. My desire is that by my life or my death, my misfortunes or my prosperity, I may contribute to the welfare of our city. Should I be successful I shall rejoice in having won peace for my country and security for myself. Should I fail, I shall know that my misfortunes were necessary for our city's good; for if our adversaries aim only at me, they will have me in their power, and if they desire more it will be made plain. If need be, I know that my fellow-citizens will unite in the defence of their liberty, and, by the favour of God, with the same success as our fathers have united in the past. I go full of hope, praying God to give me grace to perform what every citizen should at all times be ready to perform for his country. I commend myself humbly to your Excellencies of the *Signoria*. Laurentius de Medici."

The letter aroused consternation in the *Signoria* and moved its members to tears. Not many years before Ferrante had not scrupled to murder Jacopo Piccinino, who had fought against him in the Neapolitan succession war and had come to him under a safe-conduct from Milan. The thought uppermost in men's minds was whether Lorenzo would return alive. Yet the *Signoria* realized how great was the predicament in which Florence stood, and with fear in their hearts they named Lorenzo as the accredited envoy of the Republic to Naples.

Lorenzo's decision was that of a brave man and a perspicacious diplomat, but the risk which he took was smaller than appeared on the surface. Ferrante was in no position to disregard threats of a renewal of the Angevin claims on Naples which continued to emanate from the French court, causing unrest among the malcontent Neapolitan baronage. Lodovico Sforza, now in power in Milan, adhered to the tradition of friendship with Florence, and was anxious to effect a reconciliation between his two principal allies. Ferrante himself desired peace, owing to the rapid progress of Mahomet II's career of conquest, which brought the Turks dangerously near to the Apulian coast. Preliminary negotiations had been conducted between Ferrante and Lorenzo in secret, and Lorenzo journeyed to Naples on a ship sent by Ferrante to Livorno to fetch him. On his arrival, Federico of Aragon was on the quay to meet him, and another friend of his youth, Isabella, Duchess of Calabria, did all in her power to further his cause. A great admirer of Lorenzo, Diomede Carafa, who was influential at the Neapolitan court, worked for the same end. With such friends behind him and with his own unique powers of persuasion, it was not an impossible task to convince Ferrante that the common interests which had united Naples and Florence in the past were still in being. Ferrante found Lorenzo clear-sighted, peace-loving and friendly, and there is little doubt that he preferred him as an ally to Sixtus IV and his nephews.

The difficulty in the way of peace lay not with the King but with his son Alfonso and the Pope, who both strove to prevent a settlement. Alfonso hoped to increase the hold he had obtained on southern Tuscany, and

Sixtus, after loud complaints at Ferrante's treachery in negotiating with Lorenzo, insisted that the latter must come to Rome in person. The King himself warned Lorenzo that if he went he would not escape with his life from Girolamo Riario's malignity. Thus negotiations continued for many anxious weeks, their monotony being broken by balls and banquets. Lorenzo also found relaxation in pleasant walks and talks with Isabella of Calabria in the garden of her villa overlooking the sea. It was not until February 1480 that peace was signed, and Lorenzo was able to return to Florence, having achieved his purpose. As Guicciardini observed, "the terms were not unfavourable to the defeated". Florence agreed to release such members of the Pazzi family as were still in prison, and to allow the strongholds lost in southern Tuscany to remain in Sienese hands. She was also committed to giving Alfonso of Calabria a *condotta* for a term of years. This was a polite term for an indemnity, as it was plain that the troops paid for by Florentine money would not be used in the service of the Republic, and that a fresh burden was imposed on a heavily taxed people.

Although Florence rejoiced whole-heartedly at the ending of the war, the situation remained anxious throughout the summer. Sixtus agreed to the peace, as he could not fight on alone, but he refused to lift the interdict. Girolamo Riario added Forli to his possessions in Romagna by buying the city from its former lords. A revolution in Siena enabled Alfonso to win for himself a position in the Republic which resembled that of the Medici in Florence. A more direct blow to Florence was the loss of Sarzana, which fell to a surprise attack from Genoa whilst Lorenzo was in Naples, and was now in the hands of the Genoese Bank of St. George. Then suddenly in August 1480 Turkish troops occupied Otranto. Fear that the conqueror of Constantinople might soon be in Rome diverted the attention of Italian powers from their own quarrels, and the threat to Florence of enemy encirclement was removed. So opportune was the moment of the Turkish attack as to arouse suspicions that Mahomet II had timed it at Lorenzo's request. The Pope could no longer delay the reconciliation of Florence with the Church. In November a deputation composed of representatives of the foremost Florentine families—Guicciardini, Soderini, Vespucci, Capponi, Lanfredini, Tornabuoni—was sent to Rome with instructions to behave both with humility and dignity, and to reject all dishonourable demands. Kneeling before the Pope they confessed in general terms to errors of human weakness into which they might unwittingly have fallen, they listened meekly to papal reproofs for their misdeeds against the Church, and received absolution on behalf of the Florentine Republic and the whole body of citizens. As the price of pardon, Florence was ordered to furnish fifteen galleys for use against the Turks.

Meanwhile Naples had not sufficient forces to expel the invader from Apulia, and Ferrante sought frantically for aid in men and money. This was Lorenzo's opportunity. He made it plain that help from Florence would only be forthcoming if all her recent losses in southern Tuscany were restored. Alfonso had already been recalled from Siena, and orders were now sent to his lieutenant that all places occupied by the combined Neapolitan and Sienese forces during the recent campaigns should be handed over to Florence. Lorenzo responded by the gift of a subsidy of 10,000 ducats, and from that time the friendship between himself and Ferrante remained unbroken. In Florence all extolled the wisdom of one who had known how to make good, in peace, the losses sustained in war, and Lorenzo's reputation rose sky high. With the sudden death of Mahomet II in 1481, his forces evacuated Otranto. For the time being the Turkish peril had passed, and the powers of Italy were united and at peace.

Chapter Nine

Constitutional Changes

WHEN Lorenzo was free of the troubles arising from the Pazzi conspiracy, he had twelve years of life left to him—years which saw his greatest achievements in statecraft. In Florence, and within the framework of her republican constitution, his will became law both in politics and society. Outside her walls, the trust and respect with which his fellow rulers regarded him were such as to enable him to act as the arbiter of Italy. Thus he won for himself the enduring fame to which every child of the Renaissance aspired. Nevertheless, the gay and carefree spirit which marked the early years of his ascendancy had vanished. The death of Giuliano had robbed him of his closest companion, the sharer in his every interest. Although only in his early thirties, gout already held him in its grip and cut him off from much of the physical exercise in which he delighted. After the strain of war there was less money to spend on public festivities or the patronage of the arts. Life for Lorenzo became for the most part a ceaseless round of work. His diplomatic correspondence had grown very large, and he wrote much of it in his own hand. "I have been writing all day and am tired," he says in a despatch to Pietro Alamanni his representative in Rome. The constitutional and financial problems of the Florentine republic at this time called for the expenditure of much thought and energy. He had besides to keep constant watch over public opinion in the city, which fluctuated with every change in the political situation. To add to the number of his friends and to seek out and crush elements of opposition before they become dangerous, formed part of a daily routine on which the maintenance of his ascendancy depended. Yet two sources of relaxation remained to him. One was the pursuit of learning and the arts which, as he wrote to Ficino, alone enabled him to endure "the tumults of public business, and the clamours of turbulent citizens". The other was the society of his children, in whose games he shared with a zest that Machiavelli considered to be unbefitting to his dignity.

On Lorenzo's return from Naples, the first subject which called for his attention was constitutional reform. During his absence criticism of the existing régime became vocal, and a more stable basis for the authority of the Medici party was essential to its control over the government. The wave of popularity on which Lorenzo was riding after his home-coming made it possible to press through constitutional changes which would not have been accepted earlier. In April 1480 a proposal for the creation of a *Balia* was initiated in the *Signoria* and passed by the legislative councils, although contrary to custom no *Parlamento* was summoned to approve it. The *Balia* was composed of the *Signoria* and Colleges, thirty persons chosen by the *Signoria*, and two hundred and ten by the *Signoria* and the Thirty jointly. In all it numbered two hundred and seventy-seven members. Representatives of the Greater and Lesser Arts and of the four quarters of the city were included, and not more than three members of any one family might be chosen. Thus constituted, it could not fail to represent a large section of Florentine opinion.

It was given authority to carry out such reforms as seemed necessary, and eight days after it began work, the *Signoria* announced its findings. These brought about a revolutionary change in the constitution. A Council of Seventy was set up composed of the thirty original members of the *Balia* and of forty others chosen by them; future vacancies were to be filled by co-optation. The Council was given virtual control over all branches of government. It was to select the *Signoria* and Colleges, to decide what legislative measures should be put forward, and to appoint from among its own members two important new committees—the *Otto di Pratica*, which was given charge of foreign affairs, and the *Dodici Procuratori*, which was to supervise matters relating to finance and commerce. In addition it was to appoint the organ of penal jurisdiction—the *Otto di Balia*. These extensive powers were conferred on it in the first place for a period of five years, but they were renewed in 1484, in 1489, and again after Lorenzo's death. The effect of the change was to give supreme authority in the Republic to an inner ring of "*cittadini del stato*", as they came to be called, who were united in their support of the Medici. The extent to which this new body overshadowed in prestige even the *Signoria* is seen by the provision that a *Gonfaloniere di Giustizia* who had done exceptionally well during his term of office might be rewarded by a place among the Seventy. Appointment to public offices within and without the city being in their hands, members of the Seventy were able to obtain well-paid posts for themselves and their friends. Thus the prospect of private advantage as well as of civic honour acted as a magnet which drew an increasing number of citizens into the ranks of the Medici party.

Others, and among them that stout republican Alamanno Rinuccini, regarded the change with dismay. To Rinuccini, although he was a member of the *Balia* which approved it, the Council of Seventy marked the overthrow and destruction of popular liberty. For Lorenzo the Seventy served as the instrument of his personal control over the government. Himself a member of the Council, he was elected to its chief committees, notably to the *Otto di Pratica*, which was henceforth the mouth-piece of his foreign policy. The *Dodici Procuratori*, for some unapparent reason, did not become of great importance, and the management of public finance remained as before in the hands of the officials of the *Monte Comune*, of which Lorenzo soon became one. When he was away from Florence he was kept informed of the day-to-day proceedings of the Seventy by his secretary, Piero da Bibbiena. In 1481 there was a fresh plot against Lorenzo's life. It was hatched in Rome, where it seems likely that Girolamo Riario had a hand in it. The moving spirit was Giovanni Battista Frescobaldi, who had done good service as Florentine consul in Constantinople, for which, apparently, he did not consider himself sufficiently rewarded. The Florentine government laid hands on the conspirators before they were ready to act, and they were executed as traitors. A law was then passed declaring an attempt to assassinate Lorenzo to be high treason. Such was the extent to which he was recognized as the uncrowned prince of Florence.

The gravest problem which faced the rulers of Florence in 1480 was that of finance. The traditional means of raising money was by indirect taxation on goods brought into the city, and by loans from private citizens for which the customs duties provided the interest. The raising of loans was at first treated as an emergency measure, but as the expenses of government increased, the exceptional became the normal. Florentine merchants, who found it convenient to invest their money in the *Monte,* responded readily to the demands of the government, with the result that the public debt reached immense proportions. It was further swelled by the *Monte delle Dote*, or state dowry fund, instituted in 1425. Citizens made provision for the marriage of their daughters by placing a certain sum in the *Monte*, and allowing it to accumulate at a high rate of interest for fifteen years, after which the whole sum was paid out as the bride's dowry. Should the girl have died or entered a convent in the meantime, half the sum accumulated was returned to her parents or paid to her convent, and the remaining half became the property of the *Monte*. The fund was highly popular with all classes. Even Sante Bentivoglio, who had been a wool-merchant's apprentice before he was called to the first place in the government of Bologna, claimed his privilege as a Florentine citizen of providing for his daughter's dowry by this means, and after some demur was allowed to do so. In the sphere of direct taxation the *Catasto*, instituted in 1427, still held the field. This was levied on property both immovable and movable, and for the first time brought the profits of trade and industry under contribution. It was difficult to assess, particularly as the merchants, who greatly disliked it, were apt to show an expurgated edition of their books when called upon to produce them. Owing to infrequent reassessment, its incidence had come to be arbitrarily determined by the government. Now Lorenzo succeeded in replacing it by a land tax, levied on a sliding scale known as the *Decima Scalata.* It was in the circumstances probably the most equitable form of direct taxation that could be devised. The merchants, with their palaces in the city and their landed estates outside, continued to bear by far the heaviest burdens, yet they were freed from the vexations of the *Catasto*; the smaller men paid on a reduced scale. Evidence for the popularity of the *decima* appears after the fall of the Medici when there was a demand for its revival, and the government under Savonarola's influence reintroduced it in an extended form.

Lorenzo deserves credit for the initiation of a new tax, easier to assess and less open to fraud than its predecessor, but it was inadequate by itself to set Florentine finance on its feet. During the war, interest on state loans was paid, if at all, at a greatly reduced rate, and the *Monte delle Dote* was incapable of fulfilling its obligations. In 1481 a special commission on finance was set up, consisting of seventeen members, of which Lorenzo was one. It was composed of five officials of the *Monte Comune* and twelve other citizens. It was estimated then that the failure to pay out dowries as they matured had deprived the daughters of Florentine citizens of nearly half a million florins. The commission succeeded in raising enough money to pay about a third of the dowries outstanding, whilst the remainder were to bear interest at

7 per cent. until it became possible to redeem them. Ten years later the accumulation of unpaid dowries led to the appointment of yet another commission. A system was then devised by which a fifth only of the dowry was paid on marriage, whilst the remaining four-fifths received interest beginning at 3 per cent. and rising at intervals until it reached 7 per cent.; eventually the whole sum became eligible for redemption. Meanwhile the interest on state loans had fallen as low as 1 per cent., and in order to raise it the customs duties were increased. It was ordered that these should be paid in a new silver coinage known as the white farthings (*Quattrini Bianchi*) worth 25 per cent. more than the debased copper coinage still in circulation. Both this juggling with the coinage at the expense of the tax-payer and the delay in paying out dowries in full caused widespread resentment in Florence.

No other acts of Lorenzo's supremacy brought such unpopularity upon him as these. Citizens complained that their daughters were prevented from marrying in order that the house of Medici might be exalted, yet the charge that Lorenzo raided state funds in order to feather his own nest is at least unproven. Such instances of money voted to him as are recorded are for specific public purposes. His responsibility for the financial straits of the Republic at this period lies principally in the high cost of the position which he had won for himself and Florence in the diplomatic world. The maintenance of secret agents at the chief courts, the hospitality shown to foreign guests, gifts to princes and bribes to their servants were the recognized tools of diplomacy, and they imposed a burden on the Republic to which its resources were unequal. When the fortunes of the Medici were at their zenith much expenditure of this kind came from their private purse. Now that their wealth had diminished it was not unreasonable that the Republic should bear its share. Medicean diplomacy contributed to the prestige of Florence, an end near to the hearts of the citizens, and discontent was kept within bounds by pride in the reputation which the Republic enjoyed throughout the civilized world.

Thus the abuses inherent in the Florentine financial system were not eradicated. Taxes continued to be imposed when money was needed, and on those who were considered to be most likely to pay them; their entry on the books of the *Monte* as a loan served as an inadequate disguise to their true nature. Arbitrary and haphazard methods of taxation notwithstanding, there was a definite revival in prosperity before Lorenzo's death. Those of the next generation, living under a government paralysed by faction and ill-equipped to cope with the grave military and financial problems which beset it, looked back on the Laurentian age as a time of unwonted well-being. In those happy days, Florence was united and at peace, there was full employment and an abundant food supply; the wealth of the merchants and their cultivated tastes gave every opportunity for the development of talent, and throughout Italy the city was renowned as never before.

It has long been believed that towards the end of his life Lorenzo took a further step towards concentrating government in his own hands by securing the appointment of a *Balia*, composed of himself and sixteen other citizens. Guicciardini, in recording the creation of this new committee, says that it was given authority to act in matters of state as the representative of the whole people of Florence. These words suggest a body not unlike the Venetian Council of Ten, possessed of power to override the normal constitutional organs when the interests of state were involved. At the same time there were persistent rumours that Lorenzo was only awaiting his forty-fifth birthday, the age at which he would become eligible for the office of *Gonfaloniere di Giustizia*, to have himself elected not for two months but for life. Had these changes been effected, the constitution of Florence would have moved a long way in the direction of monarchy. It appears certain, however, that Guicciardini has misinterpreted the nature and functions of the Committee of Seventeen. There is documentary evidence of the appointment in 1491 of a commission on finance which, like its predecessor of 1481, was composed of seventeen members, and on which Lorenzo again served, this time as one of the representatives of the *Monte Comune*. This commission, as has been seen, made important decisions which caused a stir in the city, but its functions were limited to financial reform, and it ceased to exist when it had done its work. There is nothing to show that it, or any other body, was invested with wider or more lasting powers.

Guicciardini wrote the *Storia Fiorentina* at a time when he still hoped that Florence might have an effective system of government that was truly republican. His desire to encourage the champions of the Republic may account for a tendency, less apparent in his later works, to emphasize the despotic character of Lorenzo's rule. Possibly in the case of the Commission of 1491, family pride prompted him to magnify the importance of a body of which his father was a member. Apart from lack of evidence that the change was contemplated, the substitution of a small council with discretionary powers for the time-honoured magistracies of the Republic would have been out of keeping with the habitual respect which Lorenzo showed for constitutional forms. Not only did he fear arousing resentment among citizens devoted to the name of liberty, but he himself shared this devotion and looked upon the Republic as the destined form of government for Florence. The reforms of 1480 placed the selection of the *Signoria* and other magistracies in the hands of the Seventy, but it did not rob their members of their traditional honours and functions, and the Seventy itself had to seek renewal of its powers every five years. Lorenzo's mastery of the government could only be effected by means which left the outward form of the Republic intact. The possibility of becoming *Gonfaloniere* for life is one which he may have contemplated seriously, for this would have made him in law as well as in fact the head and spokesman of the Republic. It is characteristic of his adherence to precedent that he made no attempt to secure his election before he reached the appropriate age. Thus he never became *Gonfaloniere di Giustizia.* Dying at forty-three, his only title was that which throughout his life he had been proud to style himself—citizen of Florence.

Chapter Ten

The Peace of Italy

(1482-92)

THE last ten years of Lorenzo's life were marked by increasing tension among the Italian states, and quickened interest in Italian affairs on the part of the great European powers. Since the failure of René of Anjou to win Naples, no French prince had invaded Italy, but the bad habit of seeking French aid in Italian quarrels had not been broken. Although Louis XI abjured armed intervention, French diplomacy was active throughout his reign. Thus Frenchmen were strengthened in their impression that Italy was a prize worth conquering, and that the task would be easy, owing to her internal dissensions. Ferdinand and Isabella were now engaged in the work of unification and expansion of their Spanish kingdom, and Ferdinand as ruler of Sicily considered that he had at least as good a claim to Naples as his cousins of the illegitimate line of Aragon. He might support them against French claimants, but his own interests in the fate of the kingdom were not forgotten. The Emperor Frederick III was still the recognized suzerain of northern and central Italy, clinging tenaciously to rights which he was powerless to enforce. During Lorenzo's childhood he, the last Emperor to be crowned in Rome, had passed through Italy on his coronation journey. He treated the Sforza Dukes as usurpers, and resisted all their efforts to secure from him investiture with Milan as an imperial fief. As head of the House of Austria, he was aggrieved by Venice's expansion of her eastern frontiers to the Isonzo. Thus he had good reason to assert himself in Italy, and although he lacked either the will or the means to do so, the election of his energetic and ambitious son Maximilian as King of the Romans in 1486 brought the possibility of imperial intervention again into the picture. Added to the designs of France, Spain and the Empire upon Italy was the continued pressure of the Turk upon her eastern coasts. Mahomet II's occupation of Otranto gave disquieting proof of Italian powerlessness in the face of invasion.

Italians were not blind to the dangers from powerful neighbours to which they were exposed, and in the course of the fifteenth century they had become increasingly conscious of a common civilization worthy to be defended. Marriage alliances were contracted between the ruling families, and served as a unifying force among a people with whom family loyalty ranked high. Christenings and marriages, or the feast of a city's patron saint, were occasions for tournaments and pageantry which brought friends and relatives from all parts of Italy to take part in them. Scholars and artists moved from one centre to another, sometimes arousing ill-feeling between their respective rulers, but more often taking with them the recommendation of their own prince. The sense of a common heritage binding Italians together inspired a contemporary epigram—"Italy is a single nation, a single city, and its encircling walls are the Alps". Nevertheless, quarrels and rivalries within the Italian family did not cease. Some arose through the ambitions of individuals, but the chief source of tension was internal instability. No government was really secure; everywhere there was an element of disaffection which a neighbour's support might stimulate to open rebellion. Fear no less than ambition provoked enmity even between nominal allies. During these years Lorenzo dei Medici made his most important contribution to the preservation of Italian peace. His statesmanship taught him that to be a good Florentine was also to be a good Italian; his hold upon Florence was stronger than ever before, and he enjoyed the confidence of his fellow rulers to an increasing degree.

His achievements as a peace-maker prompted Guicciardini to compare him with the isthmus of Corinth, a piece of solid land which alone prevented turbulent seas from dashing against each other.

The peace of 1480 left Girolamo Riario breathing vengeance against Lorenzo, whom he had failed to ruin, and against Ferrante of Naples, who had deserted him. He was more than ever determined to pursue his ambitions in the states of the Church. Ercole d'Este, Duke of Ferrara, was a papal vassal, and his powerful neighbour, the Venetian Republic, had hostile intentions with regard to him. In 1482, Girolamo went to Venice to plan a joint campaign which should drive the Este from Ferrara and divide the spoils. News of impending war brought the Triple Alliance into the field in defence of Ferrarese independence. The Duke of Milan at once ordered Giovanni Bentivoglio to the scene of action, where he was welcomed as "an angel from heaven". Costanzo Sforza, Lord of Pesaro, was chosen to lead the Florentine contingent. On a raised platform in the Piazza della Signoria, he was ceremoniously presented with his baton and a banner displaying a silver lily on a crimson ground. The Duchess of Ferrara was Alfonso of Calabria's sister, and in his hurry to go to her defence he crossed the border into papal territory even before Venice finally declared war. He found his way north barred, thereby losing the opportunity of making a bid for his old ascendancy in Siena. Instead, he joined forces with the Colonna, ready as always to make capital out of the Pope's troubles, and ravaged the country up to the walls of Rome. Sixtus IV issued despairing appeals for help, in reply to which the Venetians sent their general Roberto Malatesta. He won a great victory over the Neapolitans at Campo Morto in the Pontine marshes, and entered Rome in triumph, to die there of fever. Almost at the same time Federico, Duke of Urbino, the captain-general of the allies, also succumbed to disease. The two leaders had been in conflict round Ferrara before Malatesta was called south, but comradeship in the profession of arms bound the Italian *condottieri* together by ties which no rivalry in the field could break. After their deaths, it was found that each had left the other as guardian of his family and possessions.

The first achievement of the Florentines was the taking of Città di Castello and the reinstatement of Niccolò Vitelli as its lord. This placed an old ally of Lorenzo's in a strategic position in the Tiber valley and hampered the passage of papal forces into Romagna. On the death of Malatesta, his widow and children were taken under Florentine protection lest Girolamo Riario should be tempted to seize Rimini for himself. Florentine forces also played their part in the defence of Ferrara, whilst Lorenzo carried on an active diplomatic campaign for the restoration of peace. He found an unexpected ally in Archbishop Zuccalmaglio of Carniola, who had suffered a term of imprisonment in Rome for his plain-spoken denunciation of the vices of the Curia, and then went to Basel, where he proclaimed a General Council, citing Sixtus IV to appear before it. Lorenzo sent an envoy to Basel who reported favourably of the archbishop's abilities, and said that his desire was to do all that was possible to embarrass the Pope and his nephew. "In Basel," wrote the Florentine, "the Pope is more hated than he is with us." The city continued to support the archbishop, in defiance of an interdict, and other powers showed signs of favouring him. Pisa was suggested as a place of meeting for the Council. Very soon, however, the whole scheme collapsed. The Emperor disavowed the archbishop, and the latter was put in prison, where he hanged himself in the following year. His secretary was of the opinion that he was touched in the head. The readiness of responsible people to support this crack-brained champion of the Conciliar movement showed how low the Papacy had fallen in the esteem of Europe.

Meanwhile Venice had brought Ferrara to the brink of defeat. Duke Ercole contemplated escaping to Modena, but was persuaded by the Florentine envoy to remain in his capital. The unwelcome progress of his ally alarmed Sixtus as much as the threat of a Council. In December 1482 he made a treaty with Naples, Milan and Florence for the defence of Ferrara, and called upon Venice to lay down her arms. She, however, decided to fight on single-handed rather than renounce a prize which seemed within her grasp. A congress of the allies was summoned to Cremona, early in 1483, to plan the prosecution of the war; this Lorenzo attended as the representative of Florence, notwithstanding the advice of Louis XI against exposing himself to a fresh attempt on his life by Girolamo Riario. In the struggle which followed, Venice not only held her own but attacked, sending an army into the Milanese whilst her fleet took possession of some Apulian ports. Realizing that they could not long stand alone against so many opponents, the Venetians called upon the Duke of Lorraine to come forward as an Angevin claimant to Naples, and at the same time invited the Duke of Orleans to press his claims to Milan. The invitation to Orleans put an abrupt end to Lodovico Sforza's interest in the war, and he entered into a secret understanding with Venice which culminated in the Peace of Bagnolo (August 1484). Venice alone gained by the settlement, as Ferrara was forced to yield to her the rich territory known as the Polesena of Rovigo, which brought the southern frontier of the Republic to the Po. Sixtus IV's death in the same month was popularly ascribed to his rage at the outcome of an enterprise on which he had wantonly embarked.

The War of Ferrara was a discreditable episode in the history of Italy. The unprovoked attack on a small state by two powerful neighbours, the Pope's desertion of Venice, whom Girolamo Riario had drawn into the attack, Venice's invitation to French princes to assert their claims to Naples and Milan, Lodovico's betrayal of Ferrara, the attempts of the allies to stir up the Turks against Venice, alike show pursuit of individual and temporary interests regardless of the common good of Italy or of loyalty to allies. Lorenzo himself did not come out of the ordeal unscathed. During the Pazzi war the Florentine fortress of Sarzana had been seized by the Genoese, and it was a disappointment that the terms of the Peace of Bagnolo did not provide for its return. On the pretext that the Genoese garrison of Pietrasanta had plundered a Florentine convoy on its way to Sarzanella, still held by Florence, he sent a force against Pietrasanta which besieged and captured the city. Three years later Sarzana too fell before Florentine attack. There was delirious rejoicing in Florence at this strengthening of her northern frontiers and the wiping out of the last of the reverses occasioned by the Pazzi war. Yet Lorenzo could not fail to be aware that gains in this quarter aroused enmity in Genoa and Milan. His conquests precipitated the return of a weakened Genoa to Milanese overlordship, and made Lodovico Sforza less responsive to Lorenzo's counsels of peace and friendship among the Italian powers.

On the election of Innocent VIII to the Papacy, Lorenzo expressed his opinion that the chief danger to be avoided was "another Sixtus" in St. Peter's Chair. The new Pope was the Genoese Cardinal Cibò, a man, according to the Florentine envoy, who had little experience of statecraft and would allow himself to be guided by the advice of others. Lorenzo at once cast himself for the rôle of papal mentor, but it was some time before he was able to establish his ascendancy over Innocent's wavering mind. At first papal policy was directed largely by Cardinal Giuliano della Rovere, a nephew of the late Pope, who, even at this time, showed himself as desirous of increasing the power of the Papacy by force of arms as when he became Pope Julius II. Encouraged by him, Innocent resolved to assert his authority over the Kingdom of Naples, and returned the white palfrey, sent by Ferrante as the customary gift to a new Pope in token of his suzerainty, saying that tribute should also be paid. There was rising discontent among the Neapolitan barons at Ferrante's heavy taxation and despotic policy. In 1485, Innocent constituted himself their champion and declared war, taking all available steps to stir up trouble for Ferrante at home and also to separate him from his allies.

For Lorenzo the situation was difficult in the extreme. To avoid conflict with the Pope was among his main objects, yet he could not without gross breach of faith break with Ferrante, and past experience had taught him that Naples, in the long run, was a more formidable enemy than the Papacy. He took his stand firmly on the side of his ally, pleading with Innocent on his behalf, and at the same time urging Ferrante not to provoke the Pope unnecessarily and to remove some of the outstanding grievances of the barons. Neither side, however, was in a mood to be conciliatory. Ferrante counted on an easy victory in the field, and could rely on the diplomatic backing of Spain. Innocent persuaded Venice to release Roberto San Severino from her service, and made this experienced *condottiere* captain-general of the Church. He issued a Bull of Excommunication against all who should aid Ferrante, and invited the Duke of Lorraine to come and claim Naples. There seemed every prospect of war in Italy on an extended scale. The arrival of French envoys in Florence, reminding the city of its ancient devotion to the Church, the benefits which it had received from France, and the injuries which it had lately sustained from Alfonso of Calabria, caused grave searchings of heart. Renewed papal censures and the loss of French trade were evils which the Florentines could not but contemplate with alarm. Nevertheless, the Ten of War allowed themselves to be guided by Lorenzo, and replied to the envoys in writing that they were bound by their alliance with Naples, at the same time professing their strong desire for peace and their unbroken friendship with France. Lorenzo, for his part, did not take the threat of French intervention very seriously. Indeed, he looked upon it as a useful means of inducing the Duke of Milan to honour his obligations and give active support to Ferrante. During the so-called Barons' War, Florence's share in the fighting was limited to enlisting some of Lorenzo's Orsini relatives on the side of Naples and in raising money for their payment. Meanwhile Lorenzo conducted an unremitting diplomatic campaign to keep Lodovico Sforza firm, and to prevent Venice, as well as some of the lesser Italian states, from entering the conflict on the side of the Pope.

At first the fortunes of war were with the Papacy, and Alfonso of Calabria was forced to take refuge in Tuscany; but, in May 1486, the tide turned with a decisive victory for the Neapolitans at Montorio. Lorenzo now directed his energies to inducing the combatants to come to terms. His intermediary with Innocent was Rinaldo Orsini, Archbishop of Florence, who was in the Pope's confidence, and together they brought him to realize that the policy urged on him by Della Rovere had failed. The French had not come, and the states of Italy had not rallied to the cause of the Church. Peace was signed in August, Ferrante agreeing to resume payment of tribute, and being left free to deal as he pleased with his rebel barons. Before San Severino returned north he was forced to disband his army, thereby removing a factor always liable to cause unrest.

Lorenzo was disappointed in the terms of the peace, as no mention was made of his claim to Sarzana or of the permission, for which he asked, to tax the Florentine clergy. He felt that he had been inadequately requited for efforts which had been instrumental in localizing the war and bringing it to a speedy conclusion. Yet the barrier to intimate relations between himself and Innocent VIII was now removed, and he could apply himself to establishing a dominant influence over him. The means which he adopted are known to us through a remarkable series of letters addressed to the Florentine representatives in Rome during the next few years.[1] Lorenzo wrote many of the letters himself; others are in the hand of his confidential secretary, Piero da Bibbiena. They contain detailed instructions on political questions to be brought to the Pope's notice, together with the advice to be tendered to him and the arguments calculated to influence him. No pains are spared to gratify his personal tastes. Lorenzo has learned that Innocent is fond of ortolans, so he writes that henceforth every courier from Florence will bring with him ortolans for the Pope. Another letter states that the bearer is bringing eighteen flasks of red wine of a kind which Innocent fancies, as well as some *Vernaccia*, a famous wine, over-indulgence in which had, according to Dante, condemned an earlier Pope to purgatory. In response to a request for material to make a cloak, a piece of pink cloth is sent, and a little later some damask of "matchless beauty". Lorenzo protests that he has no greater wish than to keep the Pope merry and content. As was to be expected, there are numerous letters asking for favours for Florence, the Medici and their friends. Innocent, on his side, was increasingly inclined to treat Lorenzo generously and to rely upon his judgment. A Ferrarese envoy expressed the relations between them in picturesque terms when he wrote that "the Pope slept with the eyes of the Magnifico Lorenzo". So Innocent gave ready consent to the marriage between Franceschetto Cibò and Maddalena dei Medici, and Lorenzo reaped the reward of his efforts when his son Giovanni became a cardinal.

Romagna was a perennial cause of unrest in Italy, as much from the ambitions of the greater powers to establish a foothold in the province as from the restlessness of the cities under the yoke of their ruling families. The year

[1] Cf. *Catalogue of the Medici Archives*, the property of Marquises Cosimo dei Medici and Averardo dei Medici, offered for sale at Christie's, February 4, 1918. The sale was stopped on the orders of the Italian Government and the letters concerned with diplomacy are now in the Florentine Archives.

1488 was marked by an epidemic of assassination, beginning with the murder of Girolamo Riario in Forli. After the death of Sixtus IV, Girolamo had lost his power of mischief-making, and was merely one of several petty despots, relying for support chiefly on the fact that his wife was a Sforza. His assassins were two of his captains, but the citizens of Forli detested him and seized the occasion to rebel. The populace entered the palace and sacked it, throwing Girolamo's dead body out of the window, and taking his widow and children into custody. The banner of the Church was raised in the city, but the castellan refused to yield the fortress; thus to the shouts of *Chiesa* rising in the streets, the garrison made answering cries of *Duce*. Caterina Sforza-Riario contrived to trick her captors and get into the fortress; her heroic resistance was the prime factor in saving the lordship of Forli and Imola for her young son Ottaviano. Meanwhile Milanese forces were hurrying to her aid, and the rebels did not receive the support from the Pope upon which they had reckoned. Innocent's failure to use the opportunity to bring the two cities under the direct rule of the Church bears traces of Lorenzo's influence. To the latter, the news of Riario's murder, sent him post-haste from Bologna, was not a cause of sorrow, but he knew that an attempt to assert the claims of the Papacy would have met with widespread resistance, and that the preservation of Riario rule was in the interests of Italian peace. Thus he constituted himself the champion of the Lady of Forli, bidding his envoy ask Innocent to treat her gently; whilst Caterina on her side, recognizing Lorenzo as her protector, begged him to make clear to His Holiness that she was his devoted servant. Caterina's rule lasted until she was driven from Imola and Forli by Cesare Borgia. Before this she had married Giovanni di Pierfrancesco dei Medici and borne him a son, through whom she became the ancestress of the Medici Grand Dukes of Tuscany.

A month after the crisis in Forli, Galeotto Manfredi, Lord of Faenza, was stabbed to death in his wife's bedroom by assassins whom she had engaged for the purpose. She had just cause for grievance against her husband, who had treated her shamefully, but she was a daughter of Giovanni Bentivoglio, and the prompt appearance of her father with Milanese forces in Faenza pointed to a premeditated attack on the liberties of the city in the interests of Milan and the Bentivoglio. The citizens took arms in their own defence, and, with the help of peasants from the dominion, overpowered the troops, killed the Milanese commander and took Giovanni Bentivoglio prisoner. It was reported in Rome that he, too, was killed and that all Romagna would soon be ablaze. Once more Lorenzo intervened to preserve the independence of a small state. His agent in Faenza persuaded the citizens to hand over Bentivoglio to Florentine keeping and subsequently a meeting between Lorenzo and Giovanni took place at Cafaggiolo, where a settlement was reached. In return for a guarantee of the independence of Faenza, Giovanni was released and all other Bolognese prisoners were sent home. With them went the widowed Francesca Bentivoglio, leaving her infant son Astorre, the recognized Lord of Faenza, to be brought up by the citizens. Henceforth Faenza looked to Lorenzo as the guardian of its liberty, and became virtually a protectorate of Florence.

In the course of this fatal year a plot was being laid in Bologna for the assassination of Giovanni Bentivoglio and his entire family. The prime movers in the conspiracy were the Malvezzi, members of a rival Bolognese house, who viewed the domination of the Bentivoglio with increasing resentment. They hoped to win support from outside as well as inside Bologna, and sent emissaries to sound both Lodovico Sforza and Lorenzo dei Medici. Giovanni Bentivoglio had been in the service of Milan as a *condottiere* since 1471 and his associations with Florence were also close. The predominating part which he had come to play in the politics of Romagna, and his tendency to play off one patron against the other, had not escaped the notice of either Lodovico or Lorenzo. The latter had gone out of his way to be friendly with Giovanni after the Faenza affair, but this had doubtless left suspicion in his mind as to how far he was to be trusted. As he remarked in one of his letters of advice to his agent in Rome, a ruler naturally gives more weight to one suspicion than to a hundred favours. Unmindful of the warning sent from Bologna of the plot against his father's life or of Bentivoglio's rush across the Apennines at the time of the Pazzi conspiracy, Lorenzo listened to the project laid before him with an open mind. "He consented and he did not consent" are the words in which a member of the Malvezzi family described the result of his mission. Affairs in Bologna, as far as Florence was concerned, were left to take their own course.

Plans were now laid for killing the Bentivoglio family on a November evening as they sat at supper in their splendid palace, but they became known to the intended victims through the carelessness of one of the assistants in the attack, and the Bentivoglio were saved. Lorenzo yielded to none in the warmth of his congratulations to Giovanni on his escape or in his offers of help in bringing to justice any of the Malvezzi who might take refuge in Florentine territory, and for the remainder of his life his relations with the first citizen of Bologna remained cordial. Nevertheless, the Malvezzi conspiracy and its sequel struck a fresh blow at Italian unity. The vengeance taken on those implicated and the persecution of all who bore the name of Malvezzi were even more pitiless and more prolonged than the treatment meted out to the Pazzi. Signs of sympathy with the victims, many of them innocent, showed themselves in Italy, especially in Milan, where the Malvezzi had many friends. Lodovico Sforza went so far as to say that he did not trust Giovanni Bentivoglio, and was surprised that God had protected him. Giovanni, on his side, became obsessed with the idea that his former friends were secret supporters of the Malvezzi. His own troubles, both at home and abroad, absorbed his mind, to the exclusion of the part which Bologna could play in the defence of Italy against the foreigner.

Lorenzo's main preoccupation at this time was the recurrent problem of how to avoid a breach between Naples and the Papacy. Ferrante's treatment of his rebel barons was such that some were executed, some in prison and others exiled. Their fate inflamed Innocent's indignation, already aroused by other grievances. Ferrante had not paid the promised tribute, and Alfonso had instigated a revolt in the papal town of Ascoli, near the Neapolitan border. Tension was increased by the ending of Anne of Beaujeu's regency in France, and with it of the policy of non-intervention in Italy inherited from her father. The Angevin claims had now passed to the French Crown, and the young King, Charles VIII, on becoming his own master, turned his thoughts towards a victorious expedition to Naples, which might perchance be followed by the expulsion of the Turk from Constantinople. He was encouraged in his ambitions by the Neapolitan exiles at the French court, who assured him of an easy conquest, as half the kingdom was eager to support the Angevin claimant to the throne. When the relations between Ferrante and Innocent were most strained, Charles sought papal investiture with Naples for himself. During these critical months Lorenzo's letters poured out a stream of advice to the Pope. His attitude to Ferrante should be firm and dignified, it would be a dangerous move to suppress the rebellion in Ascoli by force; he should contrive to temporize with Charles VIII without offending him; he would do well to cultivate friendly relations with the King of the Romans, who may serve "as a stick for all the dogs", as everyone in Italy is afraid of him. Early in 1492, Ferrante and Innocent came to terms. The former agreed to pay a lump sum for Naples and the latter acknowledged the Aragonese succession. It was generally recognized that this peaceful settlement was made possible by Lorenzo's efforts. A letter about this time, from Charles VIII, begging Lorenzo to use his great influence with the Pope to secure a benefice for a royal councillor, shows that his relations with Innocent were appreciated on both sides of the Alps.

For the moment Charles VIII's plans were checked, but another quarrel was brewing which was to open his way into Italy. Lodovico Sforza's relations with Naples had hitherto been intimate. He held the fief of Bari, and had taken refuge in Naples during his exile from Milan. Thus the marriage between his ward, Duke Gian Galeazzo, and Ferrante's grand-daughter was welcomed as a further strengthening of the ties between Sforza and Aragon. In fact, it had the opposite effect. Lodovico and not Gian ruled in Milan, and Isabella of Aragon was determined to play a leading part in the city to which she came as Duchess. Lorenzo was perturbed by this new cause of dissension, all the more because he, in common with the majority of Italian rulers, found Lodovico untrustworthy and difficult to handle. He assured him that he would acquiesce in any line of action on which he might decide, saying at the same time that Lodovico's proposal to marry Isabella himself and liquidate her alliance with Gian seemed to him fraught with danger. Lodovico, shortly afterwards, married Beatrice d'Este, and Isabella found herself overshadowed by a rival whose charm and vivacity made her the idol of the court. Alfonso of Calabria was fired with the wish to avenge his daughter's wrongs, and was not unmindful that his grandfather had been adopted by the last Visconti as his heir. Armed intervention from Naples to overthrow Lodovico and place the rightful Duke and Duchess in power seemed imminent. Milan, like Florence, had preserved close friendship with France, and in his extremity Lodovico turned to Charles VIII for protection. In view of the French claims on Milan, it was a dangerous move on his part, but he gambled on the fact that there was no love lost between Charles and his cousin of Orleans. He probably believed that the threat of invasion would turn Alfonso from his purpose, and that on this occasion, as so often before, the French would not come. Charles, however, saw in the quarrel between Milan and Naples the opportunity which he sought. In April 1492, the manager of the Medici bank at Lyons wrote to warn Lorenzo that the menace of a French invasion was serious. His despatch reached Florence a few days after Lorenzo's death.

Charles VIII's expedition, which proved the beginning of the end of Italian independence, cannot be treated as inevitable. Strong opposition to his plans in France kept him in two minds up to the last moment, and united opposition on the part of the Italian powers would almost certainly have turned him from his purpose. In Italy there were tentative efforts after reconciliation which Lorenzo might conceivably have made effective. As it was, the task of mediating between Milan and Naples fell into the bungling hands of his son. Charles made his victorious progress through a divided Italy, and within two years of Lorenzo's death had established himself in Naples.

Chapter Eleven

Lorenzo and his Family

IN one of the jottings with which Guicciardini filled his note-books he confesses to two main desires. The first is the continued glory and freedom of Florence, the other the renown of the Guicciardini family not only in his life-time but for ever. He, as all members of the merchant families, believed that the greatness of Florence was founded upon the prosperity of her leading citizens. Thus in his eyes his two aims were but one. The letter which Lorenzo dei Medici wrote to his son, the newly made cardinal in Rome, shows a like thought in his mind. Giovanni's endeavour, he writes, must be to help his city and his family. He must act as a chain drawing Florence and Rome together, and in so doing he will serve the interests of the house of Medici, for these are united with those of Florence. "*La casa ne va con la città*"—"house and city go together". If individualism is a mark of the age, no less is the solidarity of the family. It is reflected in the setting of daily life, in the family mansion where several generations lived in common, where the children were educated by tutors at home, and where the sayings and doings of each member were the concern of all. In his delight in the companionship of his children, Lorenzo is representative of his times. How great a deprivation the break-up of the home circle during the Pazzi war was to him is seen in his correspondence.

Clarice and her children spent the summer of 1478 at Pistoia as guests of the Panciaticchi, devoted Medicean adherents who showed them every consideration. In November they moved for greater safety to Cafaggiolo, Poliziano accompanying them as Piero's tutor. A winter shut up in an Apennine villa was no small penance to a man of Poliziano's tastes. To Lorenzo he wrote as cheerfully as he could, but in a letter to Madonna Lucrezia he unburdened himself of his griefs. The cold was intense, and he spent much of his time sitting by the fire in slippers and a greatcoat. The rain made it impossible to go out, so he instituted games of ball to give the children exercise. To add zest to the contest, the losers forfeited one course of the next meal, with the result that the game usually ended in tears. Clarice kept her husband well supplied with partridges, and filled her letters with entreaties to him to leave plague-ridden Florence and join his family. "When will Lorenzo come?" was the constant question of the children. Matters were made worse by the quarrels between Clarice and Poliziano, which ended in the departure of the latter to Fiesole in the spring of 1479. Before he left he had taught Piero to write his own letters to Lorenzo in Latin. In one, the boy says that he and his sister Lucrezia are trying who can write best; she is writing to her grandmother, he to his father, and the one who gets what he asks for will be considered the winner. Piero's request is for a long-promised pony which has not yet arrived. When at last it came he described it as "so handsome and so perfect" as to be beyond praise. Another letter gives a picture of the entire family from Lucrezia aged nine to the baby Giuliano only a few months old. "We are all well and studying," he writes. "Giovanni is able to spell. You can see for yourself how my writing is getting on. As for Greek, I work at it with Martino's help, but do not get very far. Giuliano can only laugh. Lucrezia sews, sings and reads. Maddalena knocks her head against the wall but does not hurt herself. Luigia can talk quite a lot. Contessina makes a great noise all over the house. Nothing is wanting to us but to have you here."

Piero was rather over seven when he wrote these letters, and it may be assumed that he received assistance from Martino da Comedia, who was acting as his tutor after Poliziano's departure. Their tone of easy familiarity reflects the intimacy which was considered natural between father and son.

When peace came the family were reunited, and Lorenzo was able to form his own opinion of the character and abilities of his children. Of his three sons, he said, one was foolish, one clever and one good. Owing to his failure to retain his place in Florence, Piero's folly has possibly been over-stressed. "I promise to try with all my heart to become what you wish," he once wrote to his father, and he may be said to have kept his word. In the Laurentian library a copy of Hesiod's works bears the following inscription in Greek—"This book belongs to Piero, son of Lorenzo dei Medici of Florence; his father gave it to him as a reward for his good behaviour and love of study." Piero's natural inclinations were for athletics, but in order to please his father he persevered dutifully with his classical studies and thus earned his prize. He listened, too, to Lorenzo's exhortations to behave always in a manner becoming to a citizen of Florence. After his father's death he declined the offer of the King of Naples to make him a baron, saying that he did not wish to break with the traditions of his forebears, who had never sought to be anything but private citizens. His desire to follow in Lorenzo's footsteps was genuine, but he was not clever enough to know how to do it. An Orsini rather than a Medici, he was not blessed with the wits which Cosimo was pleased to note in his grandsons. He had neither the understanding nor the tact needed to handle the people of Florence, and his tendency to swagger gave offence. The citizens, playing on the words Orsini and *orsa*, condemned his manners as "bearish".

Giovanni, the clever boy of the family, was destined from an early age for an ecclesiastical career. Before he was eight years old he received minor orders, and, owing to the title of Apostolic Protonotary conferred on him by the Pope, was henceforth known as "Messer" Giovanni. In his love of culture he was a true Medici. The books taken from the Medici library in his name testify to the variety of his literary tastes. Law, theology, the poets and orators of antiquity, works in the vernacular, in turn claimed his attention, and he was specially interested in mathematics. Yet his education did not counteract his natural tendency to dilettantism. Poliziano was soon restored to his post as Piero's tutor, but he had no responsibility for Giovanni after Clarice's insistence that the psalter and not classical texts should be used for the child's first Latin studies. Nor are there signs that Giovanni came under the influence of Marsilio Ficino. His early studies were directed by Bernardo Michelozzi, son of the architect, a man of wide interests rather than profound scholarship. Later he spent three years at the University of Pisa, where he graduated in Canon Law. Love of the arts, more particularly of music, love of pleasure and determination to avoid giving himself trouble were as characteristic of the young Giovanni as they were later of the first Medici Pope, who on his accession is reported to have said to his cousin, "Let us enjoy the Papacy, since God has given it to us." Giovanni's clerical status was from early days made to serve the interests of Florence and the Medici. Lorenzo contrived to procure benefices for his son throughout the Florentine dominion. The abbey of Passignano on the road to Siena was granted to him, as were churches at Prato, in the Arno and Tiber valleys, and in the Mugello. All were means by which the influence of the Medici was extended and landed property acquired to offset the fluctuations of trade. The King of Naples gave him the Abbey of Monte Cassino, and the Duke of Milan that of Morimondo, thus linking Florence more closely with her allies. The crowning triumph came in 1489 with the elevation of Giovanni to the rank of cardinal. Lorenzo had long cherished the ambition to have a cardinal in the family. Such an honour would place the Medici on an equality with princes such as Sforza, Este and Gonzaga, and a Florentine representative in the College would bring many advantages to the city.

Before the breach with Sixtus IV, Lorenzo had pressed for the nomination of his brother Giuliano, but the Pope could not be persuaded. Innocent VIII, more accommodating than his predecessor, was anxious to oblige Lorenzo, but Giovanni's extreme youth gave members of the College unfavourable to the Medici obvious cause for opposition. An arduous diplomatic campaign and the outlay of much money were needed before the end could be attained. At one stage the possibility was discussed of erasing from the register the date of Giovanni's baptism, and of producing witnesses to swear that he was two years older than his real age. At last came the joyful news that the cardinals, with the sole exception of the Venetian Cardinal Barbo, had agreed to the inclusion of the thirteen-year-old Giovanni among their number. "This is the greatest achievement of our house," wrote Lorenzo to his representative in Rome, adding with characteristic generosity that it was at least three-quarters due to the latter's hard work and devotion. A fly in the ointment was the Pope's decision that the new cardinal must wait for three years before entering upon his dignities. So Giovanni went to the University of Pisa, and it was not until March 1492 that he received the cardinal's hat in the *Badia* of Fiesole, and, fully robed, made a triumphal entry into Florence. Next day he heard Mass in the Cathedral in the presence of the *Signoria*, eight bishops taking part in the ceremony. Lorenzo's own end was approaching, and he was too ill to share in the festivities, but he managed to come into the hall of the Medici palace, where Cardinal Giovanni entertained the diplomatic corps and sixty leading citizens at a banquet.

The letter of advice which Lorenzo wrote to his son on his departure for Rome is a curious mixture of piety and worldly wisdom, family pride and common sense. It sums up his own philosophy of life. Of the many benefits which God has vouchsafed to the Medici, he writes, the greatest has been bestowed upon Giovanni. He must not forget that he owes his high position to no merits of his own but solely to God's goodness, and his constant endeavour must be to show his gratitude by leading an exemplary life. His first aim must be to serve the Church, and in so doing he will find many opportunities to serve Florence and the Medici. He must not neglect the good habits in which he has been brought up. Here Lorenzo expressed his pleasure at learning that Giovanni had several times been to confession and communion during the last year, without being reminded. Now in Rome, "the sink of all iniquities", he will come in contact with those jealous of his promotion who will try to destroy his reputation by encouraging him in evil ways. He must model himself upon the good and learned men who are to be found among the cardinals, being careful to avoid giving offence, and behaving always with the humility becoming in the youngest member of the College. He must shun ostentation; a few fine antiques and rare books are better worth having than jewels and silks. He is recommended to eat plain food and take much exercise, and, above all, to get up early. The habit of early rising is not only healthy, but gives an opportunity to think over and plan the business of the day. Many will ask him to intercede with the Pope on their behalf, but he should not weary His Holiness with constant requests. In his presence he should try to entertain him with pleasing conversation, and if he must needs ask a favour he should do so humbly and modestly. Giovanni replied from Rome in a letter, written in his own hand but doing little credit to his epistolary powers. The paternal pride of its recipient is expressed in the words written on the back "From my son the Cardinal".

Contemporary records have little to say about Giuliano, who was only thirteen at his father's death. There is, however, a charming description of him by Matteo Franco, when he tells how the three boys, with their cousin Giulio, illegitimate son of the elder Giuliano, rode out to the Certosa to meet their mother on her return to Florence. Both Lorenzo and Clarice had been taking the baths at Morba, from whence the former went to Pisa, leaving his wife to go home alone. As they approached the Certosa, wrote Franco, they met "Paradise full of joyous angels", that is, Messer Giovanni, Piero, Giuliano and Giulio with their attendants. On seeing their mother the boys threw themselves from their horses and rushed into her arms. Little Giuliano was looking sweet and fresh as a rose, and bright as a mirror, gay and with dreamy eyes. He asked eagerly for Lorenzo, and almost cried when he found that he was not there. In later life, Giuliano lived up to Lorenzo's epithet of a good boy, and made himself generally beloved. When the Medici returned to Florence in 1512, he was the senior layman of the family, Piero having been drowned after the battle of the Garigliano (1503), in which he had fought for France against Spain. Giuliano would have been content to live as a private citizen, but in deference to the wishes of his relations he assumed the position held by his father as acting head of the Republic. The Florentines took him to their hearts, but he was too much of a democrat to please his brother, Giovanni. When in 1513, the latter became Pope Leo X, he insisted that Giuliano should come to Rome, and that leadership in Florence should pass to Piero's son Lorenzo, whose aim was to make himself master of the city. During his years of exile, Giuliano had been an honoured guest at the court of Urbino. When he lay dying he begged Leo X not to deprive the Duke of his state, owing to the kindness he had received in Urbino when he was homeless. Leo made an evasive reply, and Giuliano had not been long dead before his nephew Lorenzo became Duke of Urbino in the place of the exiled rulers.

Of all Lorenzo's children, his eldest daughter Lucrezia was most like him in character. At an early age she gave proof of intelligence and energy. She wrote lively letters to her grandmother, the elder Lucrezia, and learned many of the latter's lauds and sonnets by heart. Among the requests which she makes in her letters are for "the basket of roses which you promised me", a sash made from the palio of St. Giovanni, and sugar-plums for her younger brothers and sisters. These are early examples of the persistency and success with which she sought favours for herself and her friends in later life. The second daughter, Maddalena, was her mother's favourite; like Clarice, she was delicate, affectionate and without intellectual interests. At the age of fourteen she was betrothed to Franceschetto Cibò, the illegitimate son of Innocent VIII, the occasion being marked by the sending of a ring to Maddalena with the papal blessing.

In the autumn of 1487 Clarice accompanied her daughter to Rome, where Innocent himself performed the marriage ceremony. The union was not happy. Cibò was a man of forty, a gambler and a profligate. Maddalena was devoted to him, and grieved over his numerous infidelities, whilst her health suffered from the late nights spent by her husband in play. In addition they were always short of money. Lorenzo gave a dowry of 4,000 ducats, twice that which he bestowed on his other daughters, and further made over to the young couple the villa which he built at Spedaletto near Volterra, but it was only after a delay of two years that Innocent made provision for his son by investing him with the fief of Anguillara with the title of Count.

The next marriage in the family was that of Piero to Alfonsina Orsini. Her father had died in the service of King Ferrante, and the marriage was celebrated by proxy in the royal palace at Naples. Piero came to fetch his bride in the spring of 1488, and at the same time Clarice, who was becoming seriously ill, returned to Florence bringing Maddalena with her. Lorenzo approved of this arrangement, as it would be a comfort to his wife, and Maddalena was too young to be left alone in the disordered state of the Cibò household. Owing to the sudden death of the third daughter, Luigia, the festivities prepared for the entry of Piero and Alfonsina into Florence had to be cancelled, but a month later, St. John Baptist's Day was celebrated with all its traditional gaiety. Cibò came to Florence for the occasion, bringing with him some Roman nobles, who were given hospitality by the *Signoria*, whilst Cibò stayed in the Palazzo Medici. He was surprised to find how plain was the fare offered to him in comparison with the lavish entertainment provided for his suite. Lorenzo explained to him that it was the custom of the Republic to entertain its guests sumptuously, but that at home simplicity was the rule and he was being treated as one of the family.

In July Clarice succumbed to her long illness, and Lorenzo was left to play the part of mother as well as father to his children. In this dual capacity he wrote in the following year from the baths of Spedaletto, where he was doing one of his frequent cures, to his youngest daughter. Contessina at the time was at home in Florence, alone with Piero's wife Alfonsina and her baby, as the Medici brothers had gone off to the country. As he hears that she is always asking after him and when he will be back, he assures his "dear little Contessina" that the baths are suiting him excellently and that he hopes very soon to return as full of health as ever he was. He hopes to find her well and happy, and meanwhile she must pray God for him and keep Alfonsina company; she must tell her from him to take great care of the baby. The boys should not have gone away and left her alone; but soon he will be with her, and then they can stay at the villa as long as they like. Contessina, aged eleven, was already betrothed to Piero Ridolfi, although the marriage did not take place until after Lorenzo's death.

Lucrezia was married to Jacopo Salviati in the autumn of 1488, an alliance which restored the friendship between the families broken by the Pazzi conspiracy. The two sisters remained in Florence during the republican period when their brothers were in exile. Niccolò Ridolfi, Contessina's father-in-law, was one of the five citizens executed for conspiring to reinstate the Medici, and Lucrezia was summoned before the *Signoria* for questioning. She spoke out boldly, saying that Piero was her brother, and that naturally she wanted him to return, indeed she had sent a good sum of money to help him. She was detained for a time, but suffered no further harm. On the accession of Cardinal Giovanni to the Papacy his sisters settled in Rome, where they competed for his favours. Their quarrels divided the family into two groups, one consisting of Lucrezia and Contessina, championed by their brother Giuliano and his friend Cardinal Bibbiena, the other of Piero's widow Alfonsina, Maddalena and her husband, with their cousin Giulio, lately created a cardinal. Lucrezia succeeded in obtaining a cardinal's hat for one of her many sons, but her greatest triumph was the marriage of her daughter Maria to the famous *condottiere*, Browning's "John of the Black Bands", whose statue can be seen today on the Piazza of San Lorenzo in Florence.

Giovanni delle Bande Nere was the son of Giovanni of the younger line of Medici, and Caterina Sforza; his son, by Maria Salviati, was Cosimo, the first Grand Duke of Tuscany. Thus the Medici who ruled over Florence until the eighteenth century trace their descent from Lorenzo as well as from his cousins. Lucrezia survived all her brothers and sisters by many years. Her later life was spent mostly in Florence, where she was venerated by her fellow-citizens as a most worthy matron. At the age of eighty she wrote a letter signed with her own hand to her grandson, Duke Cosimo. In him, ablest of sixteenth-century Italian rulers, the house of Medici reached the summit of its greatness.

Chapter Twelve

The Medici Circle

PRINCE-PATRONS such as the Dukes of Milan and the Gonzaga lords of Mantua largely determined the character of the Renaissance within their dominions. Artists and men of letters came from other cities to work there, and the court was the centre of their activities. Lorenzo dei Medici was not, in this sense, a prince-patron, and his home in the Via Larga was never a court. It was, rather, the meeting-place of friends, the resort of gifted Florentines who gained from Lorenzo discriminating appreciation of their talent and the help which made possible its development. As the Medici library was made available to scholars, so the Medici garden at San Marco, with its collection of antique statuary, was open to students of the visual arts. Here Lorenzo found the boy Michelangelo busily copying the head of a faun, having borrowed a chisel and begged a piece of marble from some masons at work there. Struck with the lad's promise, he sent for his father and arranged that he should be lodged and fed in the Medici Palace in order that he might devote himself to sculpture. It was Lorenzo's custom to take his midday meal in company with his sons, other members of the household and any guests who might drop in. The first-comers sat next to the master of the house, whatever their age or rank, and Michelangelo was among those who enjoyed this privilege. He remained in the palace during the two years which preceded Lorenzo's death, until he reached the age of eighteen, "showing", writes his biographer, "the result of his labours to the Magnifico each day". Thus he, as

Poliziano had done some twenty years earlier, owed his start in life to Lorenzo.

Florentine pre-eminence in the arts lay partly in native genius and a long tradition of culture, partly in the number of rich men who made a practice of spending money on works of art. The Medici were only one among some dozen families who decorated their houses and parish churches with frescoes, built palaces and villas and filled them with paintings and sculptures. Employment for the artist was also furnished by guilds, religious houses and other public bodies. Thus the Florentine craftsman was not limited in his work by the need to consider the tastes of a single prince, and the number of his patrons gave scope for the individuality and love of experiment which were the hall-marks of Florentine art. Natives of other cities, among them the Umbrian Perugino, came to Florence as to the "school of the world", to learn as well as to find employment. Rulers on the look-out for someone to execute an important artistic project which they had in mind turned naturally to Florence for the man they sought. About the year 1485 Lodovico Sforza, always eager to bring fresh talent to his court, commissioned an agent to report to him on the chief painters at work in Florence. The artists mentioned in the agent's reply were Sandro Botticelli, "a most excellent painter", Filippino Lippi, son of Fra Filippo and the girl whom he loved and so often painted, Perugino, and Domenico Ghirlandaio. He added that all had been employed in the decoration of Lorenzo's villa at Spedaletto. These were, in fact, the principal painters at work in Florence at the time. Antonio Pollaiuolo, who, a decade earlier, had exercised a dominating influence over Florentine painting and whom Lorenzo described as "the greatest master in the city", was now confining himself largely to sculpture. In 1489 he left Florence for Rome to execute the tomb of Sixtus IV.

Among those who remained, Botticelli had the longest and closest connexion with the Medici. His *Adoration of the Magi,* commissioned by Giovanni Lami, for the Church of Santa Maria Novella, is to some degree a portrait gallery of the family. Cosimo and Piero dei Medici kneel as Kings before the Virgin and Child in the centre, whilst on either side is a group of younger men, several of them with characteristic Medici features. Except for Botticelli himself, they cannot be identified precisely. For long it was believed that Botticelli's two most famous works —*Spring* and the *Birth of Venus*—were painted for Lorenzo. It is now established that they were executed for his rich young cousin, Lorenzo di Pierfrancesco dei Medici, to decorate the villa at Castello which he and his brother Giovanni acquired in 1477. A recent interpretation of the *Primavera* is that the subject was determined by Marsilio Ficino. The younger Lorenzo was among his favourite pupils, and in a letter to him he expounds the lessons which may be drawn from contemplation of the heavens—the sun, the moon, Jupiter, Mercury and more particularly Venus, the symbol of all the virtues embodied in the word *Humanitas.* Ficino's intention was that the *Primavera* should act as a visual incentive to the boy to cultivate Dignity, Munificence, Courtesy and other qualities on which humanist teaching laid stress. Artistic genius, however, is apt to express itself in its own way rather than to follow the lines laid down by another. Whatever Ficino may have intended, the *Primavera* transcends his purpose. In it the whole spirit of Medicean Florence finds expression—its joy in beauty, its classical culture and its quest for the unobtainable. As H. P. Horne, one of the most distinguished students of Botticelli, puts it, the Primavera is "an imaginative subject treated with great imagination". The description is no less applicable to the *Birth of Venus,* a theme suggested by Poliziano's *Stanze.*

Of the works which Botticelli is known to have executed for Lorenzo the Magnificent none has survived. The frescoes at Spedaletto were destroyed, and the "figure of a Pallas with shield and lance" listed in the inventory made of the contents of the Medici palace in 1494 has disappeared. When *Pallas taming the Centaur* was discovered in the Pitti palace in 1895, it was thought at first that this was Botticelli's lost work for Lorenzo; yet the description in the inventory does not tally with the picture, and the fact that it was known to have been at Castello points to its being the outcome of yet another commission from the younger line of Medici. Its subject is the triumph of peace and reason over brutish folly, and Pallas, wreathed with olives wears a robe embroidered with the elder Lorenzo's own crest of three rings. In all probability the picture commemorates the return of peace and prosperity to Florence during Lorenzo's last years. There is a suggestion also of an allusion to the triumph of Medicean culture over the *Pazzi* or crazy ones. Lorenzo's warm affection for Botticelli is recorded by Vasari; his patronage showed itself chiefly in the commissions from public bodies which he secured for him, among which the portrayal of the Pazzi conspirators does not stand alone. It was no doubt on Lorenzo's recommendation that Botticelli and Ghirlandaio went to Rome to work in the Sistine Chapel.

Ghirlandaio began life as a goldsmith, a training which shows itself in his careful attention to detail. This and his skill in portraiture enable him to give an unrivalled picture of the life and manners of members of the Medici circle. Two of Lorenzo's closest business associates, Francesco Sassetti, manager of the home office in Florence, and Giovanni Tornabuoni, for long manager of the bank in Rome, gave commissions to Ghirlandaio. That of the former was for the decoration of the Sassetti Chapel in Santa Trinità with scenes from the life of St. Francis; that of the latter was for a series of frescoes in the choir of Santa Maria Novella representing the lives of the Madonna and St. John Baptist. In one of the Trinità frescoes, showing Pope Honorius receiving and approving the Franciscan rule, there is an admirable portrait of Lorenzo standing with some friends and holding out his hand in greeting to Poliziano, who is ascending the stairs accompanied by the three Medici boys. In the background is seen the heart of Florence, the Piazza della Signoria with the Loggia dei Lanzi and the Palazzo Pubblico.

At Santa Maria Novella, the *Birth of the Virgin* depicts a scene in a Florentine bed-chamber when the lady of the house has given birth to a child. The mother sits upon a raised bed looking down on the baby held in the smiling nurse's arms, whilst a maid pours water into an elegant copper bowl. A party of ladies come to pay a visit of congratulation, bringing presents for the mother and child. The room with its frieze of dancing children and its painted columns, together with the choice dresses of the visitors, gives an impression of the high standard of civilization which prevailed among the Florentine magnates. For the *Angel and Zacharias in the Temple*, the setting is a Florentine church and the men wearing the red robes of citizenship who stand round the altar are known to be portraits of the Tornabuoni and their friends. The learning of Florence is represented by four men in a group apart from the others; they are Marsilio Ficino, Cristoforo Landino, Poliziano and Gentile Becchi. In the fresco of the *Visitation* there are two portraits of particular interest. One is of Lorenzo's mother, Lucrezia Tornabuoni, showing how many of her features were reproduced in her son. The other is of Giovanna Albizzi, one of the prettiest and most popular girls in Florence, who became the bride of Giovanni Tornabuoni's son Lorenzo in 1486, about the time that Ghirlandaio was working at Santa Maria Novella. She wears a magnificent dress of gold brocade and her curly hair falls from her cap. The bridegroom was a pupil of Poliziano, who dedicated one of his poems to him, and Lorenzo dei Medici played a leading part in arranging the marriage. Portraits of the young couple appear in Botticelli's frescoes, now in the Louvre. They show Lorenzo being welcomed by the seven Liberal Arts and Giovanna by the three Graces to their home at the Villa Lemmi near Careggi. Their married life, which began so prosperously, ended in tragedy. Giovanna died in childbirth and her husband was executed as a conspirator, owing to his share in the attempt to restore the Medici to Florence in 1497.

Andrea Verocchio was well launched on his career as goldsmith, sculptor and painter before Lorenzo's rise to power, but he was constantly employed by him until the artist left Florence to embark on his last work, the equestrian statue of Colleoni in Venice. The tomb in the Old Sacristy at San Lorenzo which marks the resting-place of Piero and Giovanni dei Medici was one of Lorenzo's earliest projects, and the design is Verocchio's. The urn of red porphyry, with a green plaque in the centre and a border of acanthus leaves, is at once tasteful and unostentatious. Here, in death as in life, the Medici rule of simplicity in their private concerns was observed.

About the year 1469, Leonardo da Vinci entered Verocchio's workshop as an apprentice, and first showed his promise in the angel which he painted for Verocchio's *Baptism of Christ*. According to the well-known story, the genius of his pupil decided Verocchio to paint no more pictures but to confine himself to sculpture. Leonardo continued to work in Florence, absorbing all that was best in the Florentine tradition, until in 1482 he migrated to the court of Milan. It has often been asked why Lorenzo let him go. The answer lies largely in Leonardo's inability to fit into the Florentine milieu. Merchant patrons expected their orders to be executed promptly, a requirement which Leonardo's way of working could not satisfy. His intellectual interests did not lie in the speculative mysticism of the Platonic Academy, but in natural science and mathematics, which latter subject the neo-Platonists despised. Thus on the news of Lodovico's great project for an equestrian statue of his *condottiere* father, he decided to try his fortune in Milan. Lorenzo, who knew men perhaps better than he knew how to detect outstanding merit in painting, decided to help Leonardo to do as he wished.

In order to recommend him to Lodovico he sent with him, as his personal gift, a silver lyre shaped like a horse's head; it was made by Leonardo, who played on it with great skill. In Lodovico, Leonardo found a patron who had the flair which enabled him to appreciate his gifts as an artist and also the means to allow him to experiment as he pleased in many fields. At the court of Milan he reigned as a god, transforming Milanese painting by his influence. Nurtured in Florence, his genius brought to perfection in his new home the peculiar features of Florentine art.

Shortage of money is accountable to some extent for the comparatively few commissions which Lorenzo gave to painters. His chief interest, however, lay in the field of scholarship and letters, and here he spared neither time nor expense. During his ascendancy the number of antique gems and bronzes in the Medici collection were more than doubled. Agents were employed in the hunt for books and manuscripts throughout Europe, and large sums were expended each year on their purchase. When the Duke of Ferrara asked for the loan of Alberti's treatise on architecture, Lorenzo sent his own copy, presented to him by the author, but asked that it should be returned quickly as it was a work which he frequently read. The Duke, on his side, did not show similar generosity, as he refused point-blank to lend a manuscript which Lorenzo wanted, and a Greek scribe had to be employed to copy it. Later Poliziano wrote that he had arranged for a scribe to copy "some good books", seen in Padua, "which we have not got in Florence". In Venice he was shown "a very beautiful antique earthen vase lately arrived from Greece"; he was sure Lorenzo would like it, and so had it packed for despatch to Florence.

Of all Lorenzo's friends, Poliziano was the closest. Both found their chief delight in poetry and learning; Poliziano was deeply grateful for Lorenzo's unfailing support; Lorenzo admired and loved one who could write inspired poetry and whose translation of Homer reproduced the beauty and simplicity of the original. Another intimate was Luigi Pulci, who ranks with Poliziano and Lorenzo among the three poets of the circle destined to win lasting fame. His *Morgante*, based on the French romances and the exploits of Orlando and Rinaldo, is distinguished by gaiety, wit and descriptive beauty. His poems were at times coarse in the extreme, but his dry humour delighted the frequenters of the Medici palace, and "Gigi", as he was called, stood high in the affections of its master.

A friend of a very different type was Pico, Count of Mirandola, who throughout his short life was engaged in the search for universal truth through the reconciliation of divergent systems of thought. He came to Florence after studying Canon Law at Bologna, and was at once drawn into the Medicean circle. He read Lorenzo's poetry, sought Poliziano's criticism on his own verse, and was introduced to Platonic studies by Ficino. His desire to deepen his understanding of theology led him to the University of Paris, where he endeavoured to find the link between orthodox Christianity and Jewish and Arabic philosophy. He had already studied Hebrew, and now became immersed in the hidden meaning of the Scriptures as interpreted by the Jewish *cabbala*. The *Conclusions* which he published were censured by the Church, and the *Apologia*, dedicated to Lorenzo dei Medici, in which he defended them only led to a wholesale condemnation of himself and his works. Expelled from France, Lorenzo gave him asylum in the villa of Querceto near Fiesole, and did his utmost to persuade Innocent VIII to revoke the sentence against him. But the theologians of the Papal Curia were adamant, and Pico remained under the ban of the Church until both Lorenzo and Innocent were dead, when he made a successful appeal for absolution to Alexander VI. Meanwhile he lived peacefully at Querceto, continuing his researches and enjoying the society of his Florentine friends. It was at Pico's request that Lorenzo invited Girolamo Savonarola to return to Florence in 1490. From that time Pico went frequently to San Marco to converse with the friar, whose deeply religious temperament accorded with his own. Under Savonarola's influence, he assumed the Dominican habit shortly before his death.

The common meeting-ground for men distinguished in every sphere of Florentine life was the Platonic Academy. Its members included statesmen, diplomats, lawyers, scholars, artists, musicians, doctors, who gathered at Ficino's villa of Montevecchio near Careggi to discuss problems of thought and behaviour in some degree connected with Plato. Here they indulged in the passion for conversation characteristic of the times. As a humanist writer put it—"conversation is the full perfection of learning"; "it more availeth a student to discourse one hour with his like than to study a whole day by himself". Marsilio Ficino fulfilled the task originally entrusted to him by Cosimo dei Medici, by producing a complete Latin translation of Plato's works and an exposition of his philosophic system, *Theologia platonica*, which he dedicated to Lorenzo. To him and those associated with him Platonism provided the answer to their intellectual problems and satisfied their spiritual aspirations. The principles on which these Neo-Platonists laid emphasis were first of all God as the source of truth and beauty, secondly man's desire for both knowledge and beauty, this being his distinguishing characteristic and the mark of his divine nature, thirdly contemplation of the divine as the means by which the spirit of man can attain to full development. To the Neo-Platonists religion and philosophy were sisters, for man aspires not only to know but to love and worship. They held that the contemplative life went hand in hand with the active life, and that the philosopher must live as a member of a commonwealth, being faithful and diligent in all the duties of citizenship. Education in these principles prompted Lorenzo's saying that without Platonism man could not be either a good citizen or a good Christian.

After a period of hesitation, Ficino overcame his doubts and received holy orders. He was active in his pastoral work, priding himself on being a theologian as well as a philosopher. Among his writings are some lectures on St. Paul's Epistle to the Romans; characteristic of his conception of Christianity as the fullest manifestation of one universal religion is the reference to Plato which he makes in each of his lectures. His *De Christiana Religione*, of which the Italian version was dedicated to Lorenzo, cites both prophets and sybils, pagan philosophers and Christian fathers, in proof of the verity of Christian doctrine. For Marsilio the essence of his faith lay in the fact that God became Man. Thus the Incarnate Christ is God's masterpiece, presented to man as his model. With this supreme work of art before his eyes, man, owing to his own divine nature, will be able to copy it and to become himself godlike.

A similar Platonized variant of Christianity appears in Leon Battista Alberti's book on architecture. Churches, he writes, must be planned so as to help man to know God and to know himself. Round churches are preferable, as the circle is the symbol of perfection; walls of white marble will convey the idea of purity; windows of transparent alabaster will secure the joy that comes from light and at the same time exclude outward sights distracting the mind from contemplation. Both thinkers show the humanist's faith in the power of man to attain by his own efforts to any goal which he sets before himself, an assumption which makes the process of perfection more easy and inevitable than is possible amid the conditions of a sinful world. Religion, moreover, becomes mainly an affair of the intellect, with the result that man's true end, which is the knowledge of God, is the monopoly of the philosophers. Savonarola pointed out the weakness of this conception when he said in one of his sermons, "All men, being of the same species, have the same end . . . it is not fitting that many, nay almost all men, especially children, women and peasants, should be excluded through no fault of their own from the blessedness which belongs to them".

Alberti won fame principally as an architect, and most of his life was spent away from Florence—in Rome, where he made plans for a new Renaissance city, and in Rimini, where he designed the great church of the Malatesta. Yet in his later years he returned to his native city more frequently, and, as one who aimed at covering the whole field of knowledge in his studies, he became an honoured member of the Platonic Academy. Cristoforo Landino, Professor of Rhetoric in Florence, describes in his *Disputationes Camaldulenses* a meeting of members of the Academy, at which Alberti played a leading part. The scene was the Abbey of Camaldoli, where the company spent four days as guests of the abbot, and the year was 1468. Learning was represented by Ficino, Alberti and Landino, big business by Alamanno Rinuccini, a member of a family of wool-merchants noted for its championship of republican liberty, and Donato and Piero Acciaiuoli, whose relatives traded and ruled in the Duchy of Athens until overthrown by Mahomet II. The two young men, Lorenzo and Giuliano dei Medici, together with their host brought the gathering to the ideal number of nine favoured by Neo-Platonists.

On the first day Alberti contended that the highest vocation was that of the philosopher who gave himself wholly to contemplation. He was answered by Lorenzo who urged that man should not thus separate himself from active duties. The conclusion reached was that the two could not be divorced and that the fruits of contemplation should be the guide of action. The following day was given to a discussion of the nature of the *summum bonum* between Alberti and Ficino, in which it was agreed that while there was a full perfection of good, there could be no *summum malum*, as evil was not positive but negative. During the last two days Alberti commented on the Æneid, expounding the philosophic doctrines implicit in the story. Alberti died four years later, and as he and his contemporaries passed away, their place was taken by younger men of Lorenzo's own standing. Among those united in the brotherhood of the Academy were statesmen who were found on opposing sides in the political conflicts which followed Lorenzo's death. Bernardo del Nero, of whom Ficino said that he represented the Platonic ideal of a citizen, was executed as an enemy of the Republic in 1497; Francesco Valori, one of the most ardent supporters of Savonarola and the new constitution, was killed a year later by an angry mob when the tide of opinion turned against the friar. According to Ficino it was at Lorenzo's suggestion that Plato's birthday was celebrated annually by a banquet at the *Accademia*, as the villa at Montevecchio came to be called. Nine guests were invited, Plato's *Symposium* was read aloud, and each of the company commented on some part of it. The lamp which burned before Plato's bust, the hymns sung in his honour by Ficino to his own accompaniment on the lyre, the practice of members to address Ficino as "father" and each other as "brother", and the customary greeting of *Salus in Platone*, all gave to the Academy the character of a religious confraternity united to that of a learned society. Neo-Platonism was as much a cult as a philosophy.

Academies were well known in Renaissance Italy. It was a natural tendency of the learned to meet for the discussion of themes of common interest, and court circles, where conversation on some agreed topic of intellectual or artistic significance was a favourite way of spending the evening, took on the attributes of an academy. Discussions at the court of Urbino on the qualities of a perfect courtier are immortalized in Castiglione's *Il Cortegiano*. Among the subjects of debate at the court of Milan were whether Dante or Petrarch was the greater poet, and whether Florence or Ferrara was the more beautiful city. The Platonic Academy, however, was peculiarly Florentine. Its deliberations, half philosophic, half mystical, expressed the mind of a people of boundless intellectual curiosity reaching out towards some higher good in which the spirit could find satisfaction. The informality of its organization and the welcome which it accorded to all who had something to contribute towards the discussions, whatever their age or calling, sprang from the republican tradition which made itself felt in every aspect of Florentine life. It was a source of inspiration to artists and thinkers, whilst professional men and merchants engrossed in money-making found here a way of escape from the preoccupations of their business. There is a strange contrast between the quarrels, the violence and the treachery which marked the civic relations of these Florentines and the exalted ideals which they professed as Neo-Platonists. The contemplative life of the Academy had apparently little influence upon the active life of the city. Widely separated as they may seem, each gave expression to an essential element in the Florentine nature.

Lorenzo's relations with the Platonic Academy are typical of the part which he played in the Florentine Renaissance as a whole. He was from early days Ficino's pupil, and he revered him as a father; to his fellow-members he was "brother Lorenzo". Ficino, on his side, owed his career and his home to the Medici, and Lorenzo's outstanding influence in Florence contributed not a little towards making the Academy the centre of the city's intellectual life. During his ascendancy there was no man of talent who did not reckon Lorenzo among his patrons. As a lover of music he assisted the cathedral organist, Antonio Squarcialupi, one of the outstanding musicians of the day, to obtain singers for his choir from many parts of Italy. He was primarily responsible for the portrait bust of Squarcialupi by Benedetto da Maino, erected in the cathedral at public expense, and himself composed the epitaph. The Renaissance in Florence was due not to any one man but to the creative genius of her people. Yet when Lorenzo died it was said that fortune, the adversary of genius, had deprived the artists of their best hope and support. His distinction lay not merely in encouraging artistic production but in himself contributing to it. As a poet he entered the community of artists as one of themselves. He shared with them in the striving after perfection, and his poetry was judged worthy by the most exacting standards of criticism. In the eyes of the brilliant company gathered round him, he was at once their patron, their friend and their fellow-worker.

Chapter Thirteen

Lorenzo the Poet

AMONG Lorenzo's earliest literary efforts is the letter which he wrote to Federico of Aragon, after the two had met at Pisa in 1466, accompanying the collection of Tuscan verse which he had put together at his friend's request. Here he traces the history of vernacular poetry from its home at the Sicilian court of the Emperor Frederick II, through Guido Guinizelli of Bologna, whom Dante deigned to call his father, to Guido Cavalcanti and Cino da Pistoia, exponents of the "sweet new style", and members of the circle to which Dante himself belonged. The work of these men, he contends, shows that Dante and Petrarch are not alone among Italian poets, and that there is in the vernacular a body of verse, neither poor nor rough, but rich, subtle and sweet. He concludes by saying that he is adding to the collection some songs and sonnets of his own, as a token of his friendship, and to show that Tuscan poetry still flourishes. Later, in a commentary on some of his sonnets, he champions at greater length the fitness of the vernacular to serve as a poetic medium. No one, he says, can blame him for writing in the language in which he has been born and bred. The Tuscan tongue is sweet and harmonious, and Dante, Petrarch and Boccaccio, the three great Florentine poets, have proved how well and fully it can express the manifold thoughts of the mind. Tuscan poetry, it is true, is still in its adolescence, but there is every hope that it will rise to greater perfection, especially with the increase of the power and prosperity of Florence, an end for which every good citizen must strive. The inference made here that the future of vernacular poetry depended upon the continued ascendancy of the Medici was doubtless unacceptable to their opponents; nevertheless, Lorenzo's outstanding influence in Florence, coupled with his use of Tuscan in all that he wrote, had a notable effect upon the development of Italian literature.

The enthusiasm of the humanists for the poets and orators of ancient Rome, which moved Valla to speak of Latin as "our language" and Bruni to call Cicero the father of our country and our literature, had tended to bring the use of the vernacular into disrepute. Petrarch affected to despise his Italian songs and sonnets, which could be sung by boys in the street, and there were those who belittled Dante as the poet of shoemakers and bakers. This exaggerated exaltation of Latin at the expense of Italian was already less marked in Lorenzo's day. Men who influenced him, such as Leon Battista Alberti, Cristoforo Landino and Marsilio Ficino, admired the work of the great Tuscan poets, and themselves made use of the vernacular, notably Alberti in his book on manners, *La Cura della Famiglia*. Lorenzo, unlike his masters, was not content to treat Italian as a slightly inferior alternative to Latin. A Florentine of the Florentines, his was not the poetry of the study but of the city and country-side. His aim was to express the thoughts and feelings of the people in their own language. If his example inspired his friend and contemporary Poliziano to turn from his Latin epigrams to write his *Stanze* and his sonnets in the vernacular, this in itself was no small contribution to Italian poetry.

Lorenzo wrote not for money or fame but to please himself—poetry was his solace amid the cares and vexations of government. At the same time he was a student, brought up on the classics and taking as his models not only the Latin poets, such as Ovid and Virgil, but also the great Italians. His debt to Dante and Petrarch is manifest, and his love of experiment led him to employ every Italian verse form—sonnet, *canzoniere, terza* and *ottava rima, sestina*. In addition he adopted in his carnival and dance songs and his lauds the traditional poetry of the people. In the view of most critics his poetry is inferior to that of Poliziano. The latter can sing of love with greater intensity and perfection, but Lorenzo's verse has a spontaneity, a nearness to nature and man which are lacking in the finished craftsman who was first and last a scholar. As Vernon Lee wrote in a remarkable essay, Lorenzo is the pioneer of modern "Outdoor Poetry".[1] Pastorals were well-known both before and in his day, but they sang for the most part of nymphs and shepherds in spring-time. Lorenzo found themes for his verse in the setting of the Tuscan villa, in the changing seasons, winter with its bare trees and swollen rivers, the slow return of spring, the hardships as well as the joys of peasant life. It is this new note that gives to his verse its special place in literature. To the historian, all he writes is of value as the expression of his manifold interests, the outlet for thoughts and feelings at work beneath the surface of his life in the world.

The *Comento sopra alcuni dei suoi sonetti* is modelled upon Dante's *Vita Nuova*. Each sonnet included in the collection is analysed in detail, and there are various autobiographical allusions. With the Pazzi conspiracy in his mind, he describes himself as subject to the persecutions of Fortune, attacked by powerful enemies bent on his ruin, who lay assault to his soul by means of excommunication, to his possessions, his family and his position in the state, until death itself seems to him a lesser evil. The passage is typical of the vein of bitterness and disillusionment which runs through his poetry. Besides the defence of the vernacular already mentioned, the *Comento* makes some interesting remarks on the value of the sonnet. Its difficulty renders it an excellent discipline. The writer's aim must be to present one compelling idea, gracefully, clearly and sweetly. Owing to its brevity each single word must be the right word. The harmonizing of rhyme and thought calls for great dexterity. It is equally

[1] *Euphorion*, Vol. I.

fitted to convey ideas grave and gay. The sonnets which follow show Lorenzo's capacity to rise to the standard which he set himself. The first is written on the occasion of the death of a lady much loved in Florence, in all probability Simonetta Vespucci, who was the object of Giuliano dei Medici's devotion. Lorenzo and a friend are walking together talking of their loss when they see a bright star in the sky, and the fancy that it owes its exceptional brilliance to the mingling with it of the bright eyes of the dead girl suggests the sonnet:

O chiara stella, che co'raggi tuoi
Togli alla tua vicine stelle le lume
Perchè splendi assai più del tuo costume?
Perchè con Febo ancor contender vuoi?
Forse i begli occhi qual ha tolto a noi
Morte crudel, ch'ormai troppo presume
Accolti hai in te: adorna del lor lume
Il suo bel carro a Febo chieder puoi
Presto, o nuova stella che tu sia.
Che di splendor novello adorni il cielo.
Chiamata esaudi, o nume, i voti nostri
Leva dello splendor tuo tanto via,
Che agli occhi, c'han d'eterno pianto zelo,
Sanz 'altra offension lieta ti mostri.[1]

After three further sonnets on her whose death he mourns, Lorenzo turns to the living and makes his love for Lucrezia Donati his theme. He sings of his lady's eyes, her hands, her face with its changing expression, the purple violets which become sweeter and more colourful

[1] "O bright star, whose rays rob all neighbouring stars of their light, why do you shine with such unwonted splendour, why do you rival even great Phœbus? Perhaps it is because you have taken to yourself those beauteous eyes of which cruel death has presumed to rob us; adorned with their light you can challenge the sun's chariot. O new star which fills the sky with fresh splendour, O goddess, respond quickly to our prayers, and out of thy splendour find the way to bring joy to the eyes which spend themselves in endless weeping."

because she has picked them. All are distinguished by charm, delicacy of perception and good craftsmanship, but they lack the passion of the true lover. One which is outstanding among them shows that it is nature rather than love which stirs the poet's deepest feelings:

> *Cerchi chi vuol le pompe e gli altri onori,*
> *Le piazze, i tempii e gli edifizi magni*
> *Le delizie, il tesor, quale accompagni*
> *Mille duri pensier, mille dolori.*
> *Un verde praticel pien di bei fiori,*
> *Un rivolo che l'erba intorno bagni*
> *Un augelletto che d'amor si lagni*
> *Acqueta molto meglio i nostri ardori;*
> *L'ombrose selve, i sassi e gli alti monti*
> *Gli antri oscuri, e le fere fuggitive,*
> *Qualche leggiadra ninfa paurosa,*
> *Quivi vegg'io con pensier vaghi e pronti*
> *Le belle luci come fosser vive;*
> *Qui me le toglie or una or altra cosa.*[1]

The *Selve d'Amore* in *ottava rima* take their name from the *Silvæ* of Statius. They belong to a group of poems which includes *I Amori di Venere e Marte*, the eclogues of *Corinto*, and *Apollo e Pan*, all written in the classical style natural to the cultured men of the times. Strongly as the *Selve* show the influence of the classics, Lorenzo contrives to turn them to his own purpose. He wanders through the forests of love as the spirit moves

[1] "Let him who wills seek pomp and honour, public squares, temples and great buildings, pleasures and rewards which bring with them a thousand distracting thoughts, a thousand troubles. A green meadow full of lovely flowers, a stream which washes the grass on its banks, a little bird that makes its plaint of love, these soothe our restlessness far better. There the leafy woods, the rocks, the high hills, the dark caves, the wild animals in flight and some graceful timid nymph quickly bring before my mind my love's bright eyes as if they were alive before me. Here (i.e. in the city) one thing after another robs me of them."

him, telling of the desolation of the lover during the absence of his mistress, likening her appearance to the return of spring, then turning aside to portray the dark and evil figure of jealousy, chief enemy of the joys of love. At the end comes a picture of the Golden Age, when the earth brought forth fruit of itself, when the wolf lay down with the lamb, the falcon was at peace with its prey, and man was happy because he neither knew nor desired too much. Typical of the vivid pictures of country life dispersed through the *Selve* is that of the shepherd releasing his happy flock from the shed in which they have wintered and guiding them to the high pastures and the cool streams. A little lamb trots behind its mother and one newly born is carried in the shepherd's arms, the faithful dog is guardian of them all. Even in the *Selve*, themes other than love call forth Lorenzo's most inspired verse. Platonist as he was, he believed that the love which held his lady dearer than himself, and which loved the beauty of her mind no less than that of her body, was the first rung in the ladder which ascends to God, yet it may be doubted whether he himself ever experienced the higher forms of earthly love.

In his *Altercazione*, Lorenzo expounds the Platonic doctrine of the nature of true felicity. The scene is on a hillside beneath the shade of a green bay tree with a fountain close at hand and a flowery meadow spread below. Here Lorenzo has fled from the turmoil of the city and is sitting "content with his own company" when a shepherd, Alfeo by name, asks him why he has left the manifold delights of Florence for this poor place. There follows a discussion between them on the respective joys and sorrows of town and country, of the statesman and the shepherd, bringing both to the conclusion that no one is ever content with the life he lives. Suddenly a new voice is heard, and a song sung to the accompaniment of a lyre heralds the appearance of Marsilio Ficino. Laying aside his lyre and seating himself on a stone beside the fountain, the philosopher, whom both Lorenzo and Alfeo reverence as a father, asks the former what has led him to leave his public and private responsibilities behind him. Lorenzo answers that he has sought refreshment in the pastoral life, which he envies, and begs Marsilio to tell them where lasting happiness is to be found. Marsilio replies that true felicity exists nowhere on earth but only in the knowledge and love of God.

Due ale ha la nostr' alma pura e bella,
lo intelletto e'l disio, ond' elle è ascensa
Volando al sommo Dio sopra ogni stella,
ove si ciba alla divina mensa
d'ambrosia e nettar; nè giammai vien meno
questa somma dolcezza eterna e immensa.[1]

Of the two wings, love is greater and better than knowledge, for in loving God the soul becomes divine. Marsilio's discourse ends only as the sun begins to sink, the shepherd goes to gather in his flock and Lorenzo bursts into an impassioned prayer to God, the true Light, to illuminate his eyes and kindle his heart, and thus to receive him into himself. The charm of the setting and Marsilio's lofty phrases combine to make *L'Altercazione* a true work of art. Both this poem and the *Laudi* show how strongly Lorenzo was moved by religious, and indeed Christian, sentiment. The *Laudi* were spiritual songs set to popular tunes, and intended to be sung by religious confraternities in procession or at their meetings. Their theme embraces the chief mysteries of the Christian faith. Mary, chosen to bear the Maker of all; Christ from the cross calling sinners to himself; Christ whose death overcame death; Christ giving himself, like the pelican, to be

[1] "Our soul, pure and fair, has two wings, intellect and love, on which she rises and flies above the stars to God on high. There she feasts at the divine banquet on ambrosia and nectar; nor does this supreme felicity, everlasting and all-embracing ever grow less."

his children's bread—all are sung of with a genuine fervour. Those which, perhaps, most fully express Lorenzo's inmost thoughts tell of his unsatisfied yearnings :

O Dio, o sommo bene, or come fai,
che te sol cerco e non ti truovo mai? [1]

The idea of seeking and not finding, of a soul craving for perfection which it cannot reach, runs through all his religious poems.

The Carnival in Florence was celebrated by processions and pageantry. Each guild, each age-group played its part, many staging elaborate representations of Biblical or classical scenes, and all singing their own songs. The month of May, with the weeks preceding the festival of St. John Baptist, was the season for dancing and singing in the streets and squares. Lorenzo made his contribution alike to the *Canti Carnascialeschi* and the *Canzoni a Ballo*. So entirely did he identify himself with popular poetry that his authorship of all the songs attributed to him is by no means certain. He wrote for the shoemakers, the pastry-cooks, the bakers, for vendors of oil and perfumes, gold-thread spinners, muleteers, country-women selling cucumbers and water-melons; even the scavengers and the beggars were not forgotten. To read his songs is to mingle in the noisy crowd of the Carnival, where young and old are bent on merry-making and on extracting every ounce of enjoyment from the day's holiday, when poverty and toil can be forgotten. The song of the mother giving advice to her daughter, and the daughter's story of how she acts upon it, reflect the low moral standards of the times, as does the altercation between old husbands and young wives. All abound in coarse jokes and innuendoes. Their underlying motif is, however, that of the transitory nature of youth and happiness, a thought

[1] "O God, O highest good, how is it that I seek thee only and never find thee?"

which finds expression in the most famous of Lorenzo's songs. *Giovinezza* was written to accompany a representation of the triumph of Bacchus. It was appropriated by the Fascists as their national anthem and altered for their purposes. In its original it is the very essence of the Carnival as seen through Lorenzo's eyes.

> *Quant' è bella giovinezza*
> *Che si fugge tuttavia!*
> *Chi vuol esser lieto, sia;*
> *Di doman non c'è certezza.*[1]

I Beoni (The Drunkards) is at once a satire on drink and a parody of the Divine Comedy, written in Dante's *terza rima*. Lorenzo's journey is not through the other world but to Ponte a Rifredi, a little way outside Florence. He tells how, on an autumn day, he was returning to the city when he met an eager crowd hurrying in the opposite direction. Seeing a friend, one Bartolino, he asked whither he was bound, and learned that a barrel of good wine had been broached at Ponte a Rifredi and that all were going to drink of it. Lorenzo turns in the same direction, and Bartolino acts as Virgil to his Dante, pointing out various individuals in the company and engaging them in conversation. Among them are members of leading Florentine families and several priests, as well as men of low degree. Each carries his cup, and all are united in their praise of drink. *I Beoni* contains lively portraits, such as that of the long-nosed priest of Fiesole who has made drink his paradise, and the man who has provided himself with a dried herring and some anchovies in order to stimulate thirst. There is a rollicking gaiety about the poem, but there are also profanities which rival the worst specimens of Renaissance verse. What induced an ardent Dantist to write it remains a mystery. Possibly

[1] "How fair is youth, and how fast it flies away. Let him who will be merry, of tomorrow naught is sure."

Lorenzo became disgusted with his own work, for the last *capitolo* breaks off abruptly before the drinking has begun.

In his later years Lorenzo produced a play—*La Rappresentazione di San Giovanni e Paolo*—which was acted in 1489 by the Company of St. John the Evangelist, a confraternity of boys. The ten-year-old Giuliano dei Medici was in the cast, and it has been suggested that Lorenzo himself took the parts of the Emperors Constantine and Julian. Like the numerous *sacre rappresentazioni*, or morality plays, on which it was modelled, it takes the form of a series of disconnected scenes; it has the appearance of verses hastily put together for the young actors, who plead indulgence for their performance on the ground of their tender years. The first scene introduces Costanza, daughter of the Emperor Constantine, who, on being cured of leprosy by the prayers of St. Agnes, resolves to become a nun. Her hand, however, is claimed by an imperial general, Gallicano, as his promised reward for victory over the Persians. Both father and daughter are reluctant to agree to the marriage, yet there is no suggestion of any incongruity in the behaviour of the saintly Costanza when she proposes that Constantine, while expressing his pleasure at having Gallicano as a son-in-law, should send him on a dangerous mission from which he is unlikely to return alive. Constantine praises his daughter's ingenuity for finding a way out of the dilemma which will save his honour. Gallicano accepts the charge placed upon him, and sets out to subdue Dacia, taking with him two young Christian soldiers, Giovanni and Paolo. Through their prayers defeat is turned into victory. Gallicano is converted, the army goes into battle under the standard of the Cross, the King of Dacia is made prisoner and his city taken. On returning to the court, Gallicano announces that the victory was not his but Christ's, and that he desires to leave the world and serve God. Thus Constanza is free to follow her vocation. Constantine now decides to abdicate, and his eldest son assumes power. The latter's reign is short and troubled, and he dies ascribing his misfortunes to the toleration granted to Christians. On the election of his cousin, Julian the Apostate, as Emperor, a fierce persecution of Christians follows, in which Giovanni and Paolo are among those who suffer martyrdom. Relief comes when St. Mercurio is raised from the grave and inflicts a mortal wound on the Emperor as he rides in the midst of his armies. Julian acknowledges that in him many Christians have been avenged, and dies with the traditional words on his lips, "O Cristo, Galileo, tu hai pur vinto". [1]

The play is memorable chiefly for Constantine's speech on laying down his office, an occasion which Lorenzo uses to express his own ideas on government. The sweets of power he declares exist only in appearance; trouble and fatigue of body and mind are in truth the ruler's lot. In order to maintain his authority, he must not consider his own advantage but the general good. He must keep an increasing watch over public opinion, he must shun luxury and avarice, and be kind and gracious. He must set a good example, as all eyes are turned upon him. The ruler, in short, must be the servant of servants. Julian the Apostate is made to strike the same note when he describes the ruler as a distributor not an owner. The wealth of the Empire belongs to the people, and it is the Emperor's responsibility to see that all are fed and cared for. Honour is his sole reward. Lorenzo's repudiation of the practice current in his day of consulting the stars in times of crisis finds expression in Julian's refusal to listen to his astrologers.

Il re e'l savio son sopra le stelle
Ond'io son fuor di questa vana legge:
I buoni punti e le buone ore son quelle
Che l'uomo felice da se elegge.[2]

[1] "O Christ, Galilean, thou hast conquered."
[2] "The king and the sage are above the stars, thus I dissociate myself from this vain custom. Good moves and good moments are those which the fortunate man chooses for himself."

Among three poems which rank as Lorenzo's masterpieces, *La Nencia di Barberina* is perhaps the most finished. It is a story of a peasant's love, but not that of a loutish Corin for an ill-favoured Audrey. Vallera is a prosperous young farmer, paying rent for land and appliances in the form of half the produce, according to the *mezzeria* system familiar to Lorenzo from his childhood and still common today. He goes to Florence to sell two mules, and offers to bring back to his Nencia anything that she fancies, from pins and buttons to a bead necklace or a silk scarf. Nencia, the shepherdess, when she goes in her best clothes to Mass on Sunday, seems like a pearl in her lover's eyes. At a dance she is nimble as a goat, she whirls round like a mill-wheel, and, when it is over, her curtsy is as graceful as that of any fine lady in Florence. All Vallera's comparisons are taken from familiar features of his daily life. Nencia is soft as lard and white as flour; she is clearer than water from the fountain and shines like a star rising over the roof. Yet Lorenzo contrives to express through each homely simile Vallera's deep love.

Non ho potuto stanotte dormire
mill' anni me parea che fusse giorno,
per poter via con le bestie venire,
con elle insieme col tuo viso adorno.
Epur del letto me convenne uscire:
puosimi sotto'l portico del forno
e livi stetti pùi d'un'ora e mezzo
finchè la luna se ripuose al rezzo
Quand'i te vìdi uscir della capanna
Col cane innanzi e colle pecorelle,
e' me ricrebbe el cuor pùi d'una spanna
e le lacrime vennon pelle pelle.

He cannot sleep at night, and it seems a thousand years before dawn breaks and Nencia will come out with her flock. He waits outside the bake-house for more than an hour and a half, until the moon fades. When at last she comes with her sheep, the dog leading the way, his heart leaps and the hot tears fall. If she were to drive a knife into his heart, he concludes, it would cry out "*Nencia, Nencia bella*". Lorenzo's entry into the mind and feelings of Vallera is something which other poets of his day could not, nor indeed cared to do. When Pulci tried to imitate *La Nencia,* he produced a burlesque. Lorenzo wrote an enchanting love poem.

In *La Caccia con Falcóne* Lorenzo lives again the joys of a day's hunting in which he delighted. The poem opens with a lovely description of the start in early morning, when the east is aglow and the hills are tipped with gold, when the stars are disappearing, the wolves and the foxes have slunk away to their lairs, and the peasants are going to work. Then the huntsmen appear with hawks, falcons and dogs, the names of the last being all recorded. The dogs putting up the game, the falcons swooping on their prey, the galloping horses are described, as is a quarrel and its mending between two rival hawkers. So the time passes until the tired riders begin to think of home, and they return to relive the events of the day in their dreams. In *La Caccia* Lorenzo has freed his mind from the cares and vexations of statecraft and has become for the time being the complete huntsman.

Ambra commemorates Lorenzo's villa at Poggio a Caiano, situated near the junction of the Ombrone with the Arno. The story is modelled on Ovid's *Metamorphoses,* and tells of the nymph Ambra beloved by the shepherd Lauro (Lorenzo) and also by the river god Ombrone. She flies before Ombrone's pursuit until her way is barred by his comrade Arno, whereupon she persuades the goddess Diana to change her into a rock. There she remains, a small island encircled by her proud lover, who continues to bewail her loss. *Ambra* consists of two loosely connected parts. The first describes, in Lorenzo's best vein, the country in winter when the harvest is garnered

—the migrant birds have gone overseas, the trees are bare and the rivers swollen. As the floods rise the frightened peasant frees his beasts from their stalls and seeks safety, carrying his goods on his back and his weeping child in his arms.

Alcun della famiglia s'è ridotto
in cima delle case; e su d'al tetto
la povera ricchezza vede ir sotto,
la fatica, la speme; e per sospetto
di se stesso non duolsi e non fa motto;
teme alla vita il cor nel tristo petto,
nè delle cose car par conto faccia;
cosi la maggior cura ogni altra caccia.[1]

In the second part the adventures of Ambra and her lovers are told charmingly enough, but they come as something of an anti-climax to the realistic picture of the flood.

The two volumes of Lorenzo's collected poems constitute no mean achievement for one who could only be a poet in his scanty hours of leisure. Here each aspect of his many-sided nature finds expression; he writes in turn as lover, scholar, statesman, philosopher, countryman, as one who revels in the joy of living and at the same time is haunted by abiding melancholy. He is too eclectic and too much occupied in experimenting in the different forms of poetry known to him to lay claim to originality. He is individual, however, in his intimate knowledge and love of the Florentine people and the Florentine landscape. He can write of the olive leaves, now white, now

[1] "Some people take refuge at the top of their houses, and from the roof see their poor wealth being carried away, and with it their toil and their hope; anxious for their own safety they neither lament nor speak. The heart in each sad breast fears for life and seems to take no heed of cherished possessions, the greater trouble drives out all others."

green, as they are tossed from side to side by the winter wind, of the shepherd and his dog as they tend their flock, of the pastry-cook commending his wares to the Carnival crowd, because all are objects of his observation and delight. Herein lies his distinction as a poet.

Chapter Fourteen

Death of Lorenzo

As a boy Lorenzo was strong, active and healthy, but signs of the malady which afflicted him began to show themselves even before his accession to power. He inherited his father's gouty tendency, but his main trouble appears to have been arthritis, accompanied by bouts of rheumatic fever, causing increasing failure of bodily power as well as much pain. Like the majority of his contemporaries, he was a great frequenter of baths. Visits to the bathing establishment founded by his mother at Morba, to Spedaletto where he had a villa, or to Porretta, the favourite resort of the rank and fashion of Bologna, became an annual event. He returned from his cures with cheerful optimism, pronouncing himself to be "fresh and well" and "full of health". Nevertheless, his debility increased until he could not walk or hold a pen. His favourite country residence after he had parted with Cafaggiolo was the villa at Poggio a Caiano, which he acquired in 1480 and named *Ambra*. It was rebuilt for him by Giulano di San Gallo, and Andrea del Sarto was among the painters employed to decorate it. Here he interested himself in agricultural experiments, and in the animals presented to him by the Sultan of Babylon, which were kept there. These included apes, parrots and a giraffe "so gentle that it will take an apple from the hand of a child". Some representatives of the Sultan's gift, together with classical scenes, figure among the frescoes in the villa. An inventory of the books in Lorenzo's bedroom here show the literary works to which he turned for refreshment in his later years. It includes the Gospels, the works of the three great Florentine poets,

Dante, Petrarch and Boccaccio, the Consolations of Bœthius, a treatise on medicine and the sonnets of Burchiello. In the burlesque verses of this barber-poet, who died in the year of Lorenzo's birth, the sorrows and the laughter of a Florentine son of the people live again. Poggio a Caiano lay within easy reach of Florence, on the road to Pistoia, but as movement became more difficult Lorenzo made his country home at Careggi, from whence he could ride or be carried in a litter to the city. Various strange remedies were prescribed for him. Among them was a stone called heliotrope set in gold in such a way as to touch the skin, to be worn as a ring on the left hand; with this, it was claimed, gout and arthritic pains would never return. As a last resort he was given a mixture of precious stones pounded in a mortar. Ser Piero Leoni, his favourite doctor, gave more practical advice when he told him to beware of cold and damp feet and the air at sunset, and not to eat pears or swallow grape pips. He, however, after Lorenzo's death was blamed for his lying sciences, allied to necromancy, and in his grief and distress committed suicide by throwing himself into a well.

After saying farewell to his son the cardinal before he set out for Rome, Lorenzo left Florence for the last time. The incidents of his death-bed at Careggi are described by Poliziano, who was with him to the end, in a letter written some six weeks later. When he knew that death was approaching, he sent for a priest and made his confession. On hearing that the Last Sacrament was being brought to him he insisted upon rising, saying that he desired to go and meet the Lord who had created and saved him. He fell on his knees and prayed until the priest ordered his attendants to help him back to bed, where he received his viaticum in great peace and devotion. He next had a farewell talk with his eldest son, to whom he spoke words of comfort and advice. Hearing Poliziano's voice, he called out "Are you here, Angelo?", and as his friend approached, took both his hands, pressing them between his own. Pico della Mirandola hastened out to Careggi on hearing that Lorenzo had expressed a wish to see him. To him Lorenzo said that he died more willingly after seeing so great a friend, adding half jokingly, "I wish that death had spared me until I had finished collecting your library". The next visitor to come, also at Lorenzo's request, was Girolamo Savonarola. According to Poliziano's account, Savonarola exhorted the sick man to hold fast to his faith, to amend his life if he should be spared and if not to accept death as the will of God. Lorenzo gave whole-hearted assent to all that was urged upon him, and before Savonarola left asked for and received his blessing. During his last hours the Passion of Christ was read to him, and he lay listening, pressing a silver crucifix to his lips from time to time, until on the night of Sunday, April 8, 1492, he departed from this life.

A very different story of the interview between Savonarola and Lorenzo is told by Cinozzi, on the authority of Fra Silvestro, one of the Dominicans who died with his Superior, and who, according to Cinozzi, heard it from Savonarola's own lips. Here Lorenzo is represented as saying that there were three sins on his conscience for which he desired absolution, the sack of Volterra, the robbery of the *Monte delle Dote* and the cruel vengeance taken on the Pazzi. Savonarola replied that God was merciful, but that three things were needful on Lorenzo's part. The first was faith, to which Lorenzo replied, as in Poliziano's narrative, that he had the fullest faith in God's mercy. Secondly, he must give instructions for the restoration of his ill-gotten wealth, and to this Lorenzo after some hesitation assented. Thirdly, he must restore liberty to Florence. On these words Lorenzo turned his back on the friar and remained silent; Savonarola left without absolving him and soon after Lorenzo died, tortured by remorse. This sensational story, recorded some eight years after the event, was repeated by Savonarolist adherents, notably by the friar's principal biographer Burlamacchi, and has figured widely in popular narratives. Historians, recognizing that neither Poliziano nor Cinozzi could be considered free from bias, have hitherto adopted whichever version coincided with their own estimate of Lorenzo's character. In recent years, however, the discovery by Professor Ridolfi of a letter from an unprejudiced source, written five days after Lorenzo's death, substantiates the truth of Poliziano's statements. Carlo del Benoni, writing to give his friend Piero Guicciardini the news of Florence during his absence on official business at Pisa, records the death of "the common father of our city", adding that he had received all the sacraments and had been seen by Savonarola, "from whose visit he derived much comfort". Finally he expresses the opinion that Lorenzo was as admirable in the manner of his death as he had been in life.[1]

Apart from the question of evidence, there are inherent improbabilities in the Savonarolist legend. It is in the first place difficult to credit that Lorenzo, having already made his confession to his parish priest, on which point all accounts agree, should wish to make a second confession to Savonarola. Again, the attempt to depict the death-bed interview between Lorenzo and Savonarola as the clash between two opposing principles of tyranny and civic freedom is to ante-date the part played by Savonarola in Florentine politics. When he first came to the Convent of San Marco as lector in 1482 his preaching failed to attract the critical Florentines. So little impression did he make when he preached in San Lorenzo that only twenty-five women and children were there to hear him by the end of his course. His great reputation as a preacher dates from 1490, when after some years' absence he was sent back to San Marco, on a request to the General of his order, made by Lorenzo at the instance of Pico della Mirandola. His first course of sermons in the Duomo in 1491 was attended by enthusiastic hearers drawn from every class and interest in the city. The intellectuals appreciated his learning, his philosophical outlook and his power of relating Biblical teaching to

[1] Ridolfi, R., *Studi Savonaroliani*, 1935.

practical life. His denunciation of vice and his prophecies of the scourge about to fall upon Italy, and the regeneration which would follow, made an immense popular appeal. Lorenzo was among the many who recognized him as a true man of religion. The only criticism on Savonarola he is known to have made is when, fearing the effect of his prophecies on the excitable Florentines, he sent a message telling him to talk less about the future. San Marco was closely associated with the Medici, and the Lent and Advent preaching in the Duomo was arranged by the *Signoria*. Thus Lorenzo could easily have silenced Savonarola, or caused him to be transferred from San Marco, if he had considered him dangerous to the maintenance of his own supremacy. Far from taking steps to suppress him, he turned to him for consolation when he was dying. The part played by Savonarola in the internal politics of Florence did not, in fact, begin until after the expulsion of the Medici. Then, when his prophecies seemed fulfilled by the presence of the French invader, the people turned to him as their guide, and a democratic constitution was set up through his influence. Henceforth, the maintenance and strengthening of the new régime became one of the principal subjects of his preaching, and he took every opportunity to emphasize the contrast between past tyranny and present liberty. Thus he vested Lorenzo in the garb of a tyrant, and his followers embroidered on the theme, without asking themselves by what possible action could Lorenzo, at the hour of his death, have restored liberty to Florence.

Lorenzo's body was brought from Careggi into Florence to await in the convent of San Marco its burial in the Medici church of San Lorenzo. It was laid in the Old Sacristy until in the sixteenth century it was transferred, together with remains of his brother Giuliano, to the New Sacristy built by Michelangelo for Pope Clement VII. According to the original scheme there were to be four great sepulchral monuments in the sacristy, representing Lorenzo's son and grandson and, in all probability,

Lorenzo himself and his brother. Two only were completed. Michelangelo's art as a sculptor reached its consummation in the statues of the younger Giuliano and Lorenzo, the two Medici who returned to the chief place in Florence in 1512. Lorenzo Il Magnifico and the elder Giuliano rest in a nameless grave.

A few days after Lorenzo's death a proposal by the *Signoria* that Piero should succeed to all the offices held by his father was passed through the Councils by a majority of seven to one. The step was, in the words of the decree embodying it, "a public testimonial of gratitude" to the memory of a great man "who subordinated his personal interests to the good of the community". The votes recorded are probably a fair indication of the feeling of the citizen class. Among the merchant oligarchy there was a hard core of resistance to Medici domination, but the great majority, including some who had fallen under Lorenzo's displeasure, realized that the surest guarantee of the unity on which their power depended lay in the ascendancy of one man. Thus they resolved in their own interests to continue the unofficial dictatorship under which Florence had lived for nearly sixty years. Of genuine mourning for Lorenzo in all ranks of society there is abundant testimony. The poorer classes bewailed the loss of a liberal benefactor, and one who provided them with numerous forms of entertainment. Artists and men of letters were deprived of unfailing and enlightened support. The letters of condolence which poured in from Italian and European powers brought home to the citizens the esteem in which Lorenzo was held throughout the civilized world. No one showed deeper regret nor greater apprehension for the future than Ferrante of Naples when he wrote : "This man has lived long enough for his own immortal fame but not for Italy. God grant that now he is dead men may not attempt that which they dared not do while he lived." Popular opinion in Florence is summed up by the chemist Landucci, who recorded in his diary that Lorenzo was the most glorious man that could be found: "All men say that he guided Italy, for indeed his head was wise and all his schemes had good success." Appreciation of Lorenzo's achievements caused the Florentines to turn a blind eye on the fact that under him their cherished liberty existed in name only. Yet the forms of republican government remained, and with them the power to dispense with a leader, who in the opinion of those in authority no longer promoted the general good.

Piero appears at first to have done his best to give satisfaction. Acknowledging his youth and inexperience, he expressed his intention to be guided by the advice of the leading citizens in matters of state. Yet his extravagances and the number of his horses and falcons befitted a prince rather than a private citizen, and the time he spent in sport, to the neglect of public business, aroused criticism. Thus Florence reserved judgment upon him. The crisis came when, all efforts at appeasement between Milan and Naples having failed, Lodovico promised his support to Charles VIII. Thus the hope of preventing a French invasion of Italy vanished, and Florence had to choose between breaking with France, her age-long ally as well as her best customer, or deserting the King of Naples, whom she was pledged to aid against aggression. Piero, with the full support of the government, decided to stand by Naples, but he could not carry the city with him. Workers in the wool trade were thrown out of employment by a French embargo on Florentine goods. Lorenzo and Giovanni dei Medici, Piero's cousins, were discovered to be in secret communication with France, and were sent out of the city. The voice of public opinion pronounced that Florence should side with France and Milan, and not with Naples. When, in the autumn of 1494, the French army was descending upon Tuscany, resistance melting on its approach, Piero made a desperate effort to save the situation. Possibly having in mind his father's famous journey to Naples in search of peace, he went secretly to the French camp to negotiate with

Charles. The outcome of the interview was the unconditional surrender of four Florentine fortresses—Pisa, Livorno, Sarzana and Pietrasanta—to the French, thus opening to them the way to Florence. Horrified at the news, the *Signoria* decided that Piero's supremacy was contrary to the public interest, and should there and then be ended. On his return to the city, he found the doors of the Palazzo Vecchio shut against him, and that night he was riding over the Apennines to Bologna, never to see Florence again.

The rapidity and ease with which he was ousted gave dramatic proof of the dependence of the Medicean supremacy upon the consent of the chief magistracy of the Republic. There followed eighteen years of experiment in a form of government resting on a broader basis. Its chief feature was a Grand Council on the Venetian model, which won the approval of the leading political theorists of the day, and at first worked well. Owing largely to Savonarola's intervention, the constitutional change was effected without bloodshed, and Charles VIII entered Florence as a friend. All too soon, however, faction showed its head. Many members of the merchant oligarchy, who had hoped to retain their power after they had dispensed with the Medici, were opposed to a system which brought the middle classes into greater prominence. The Grand Council became a battlefield between oligarchs and democrats and an obstacle in the way of effective government. After a year or so, the moral and religious fervour inspired by Savonarola produced a violent reaction, and served only to embitter the civic strife which the friar had striven to heal. His martyrdom in 1498 led to no fundamental change in the internal or external situation of the Republic. The election of Piero Soderini as *Gonfaloniere di Giustizia* for life failed to put an end to faction, and the French alliance not only involved Florence in much expense but isolated her from the other Italian powers when they united to drive out the foreigner. Increasing difficulty in raising money and rebellion in the subject cities added to the troubles of the government.

The end came in 1512 when Louis XII of France was driven from Milan, the army of the Holy League marched on Florence, Piero Soderini fled and the Medici returned. Guicciardini was among those who hoped that the reforms of 1494 would create "a well-ordered Republic" in Florence. Recognizing that his hopes had been misplaced, he now wrote a tract setting out the means by which the Medici might re-establish their authority. His chief word of advice was that they should conduct themselves after the manner of "the old Lorenzo". About the same time Machiavelli wrote his *Prince*, dedicated to the younger Lorenzo, calling upon him to impose unity upon Florence and to become the saviour of Italy, by leading a campaign for the expulsion of the foreigner.

Guicciardini and Machiavelli, alike republicans at heart, here show their recognition of the work which Lorenzo Il Magnifico had accomplished. The tragedy of the Florentines lay in their passionate republicanism coupled with a spirit of faction which paralysed any government in which a large body of citizens had effective share. "Truly this evil which besets us is in ourselves" it was said early in the fifteenth century in the course of a long discussion on how to deal with quarrels among citizens. During Lorenzo's ascendancy the problem was so far solved that Florence had a strong government while her cherished republican institutions were preserved. From his own age until today there have been those who called Lorenzo a tyrant; yet the term is hardly applicable to one who had no armed support, and who was dependent for his authority on the consent of the chief magistracy of the Republic. How he managed to keep control over the government and to secure a sufficient majority in the Councils for measures which he considered expedient must always remain something of a mystery. His methods combined ruthlessness with tact. All were made to realize the benefits accruing from his friendship and the dangers to which those who opposed his will exposed themselves. The same capacity to reconcile irreconcilables is seen in his foreign relations, where he worked unceasingly for Italian unity, and at the same time did his utmost to preserve the independence of those small states from which arose the rich variety of Italian civilization. Only a man of his peculiar character and gifts could fill the place which he filled, either in Florence or in Italy. His successors proved wholly incapable of so doing. The drift towards monarchy was already visible before the last Florentine Republic went down before the combined armies of Empire and Papacy in 1530. From that time the Medici ruled first as Dukes of Florence and later as Grand Dukes of Tuscany, and Italy was subject to foreign domination.

Lorenzo was a child of his age alike in his deep love of beauty and learning and in his refusal to allow moral considerations to stand in the way of political and personal aims. Any action was justified in his eyes which served the interests of Florence and the Medici. He was by nature opposed to violence, and the sack of Volterra, together with the vengeance meted out to the Pazzi, continued to weigh upon his mind. Nevertheless, he was responsible for the chain of events which led to the former outrage, and he did nothing to check the latter. As an enemy he was unforgiving, but he was a good friend. He was unremitting in furthering the interests of those who won his affection, and showed generous recognition of services rendered to him. His intense interest in and understanding of his fellow-men enabled him to gain the confidence of an Innocent VIII or a King Ferrante, to enjoy the friendship of men of such different temperaments as Pulci and Pico della Mirandola, and to enter into the feelings of Florentine artisans and Tuscan peasants. Perhaps his greatest gift is best expressed in the word *civiltà*, the capacity to live as a citizen among citizens. He never gave himself airs, even his children called him Lorenzo. When in company with a citizen older than himself, he was careful to give him the place of honour on his right hand. During his ascendancy, Florentine society remained republican in spirit and united. Politics, big business, learning and the arts were not separate worlds, but a single whole, through which Lorenzo moved as one who shared in its every aspect. The stimulating effect of such an environment on men of talent and enterprise cannot easily be over-estimated. Common ideals, criticism both outspoken and intelligent, fierce competition and boundless opportunity bore fruit in great creative work. The most brilliant period of Florentine history is that which bears the name of the Laurentian age.

Chapter Fifteen

Florence and the Italian Renaissance

TO many minds the term Italian Renaissance suggests first of all Florence and the Medici. Such a point of view was fostered in England by the Liverpool lawyer William Roscoe, whose pioneer work on Lorenzo dei Medici was published in 1796. Unable to go to Italy himself, he collected all the printed books on which he could lay hands, and had manuscripts in the Florentine archives and libraries copied for him by a friend. These included many of Lorenzo's letters and much of his poetry hitherto unpublished. His aim was to write not only of historical events but of the progress of letters and the arts. His realization of the intimate connexion between politics and culture is the outstanding merit of Roscoe's work. In his eyes Lorenzo was "perhaps, on the whole, the most extraordinary man that any age or nation has produced". Through him he gained his introduction to the Italian Renaissance, and he was so dazzled by the splendours of the Medicean age that he failed to grasp either that the Renaissance in Florence had its origins before the Medici rose to power, or the extent to which the spirit of the Renaissance was alive in other Italian cities.

As regards Florence, three of her most famous buildings—the Cathedral, the Palazzo Vecchio and the Franciscan Church of Santa Croce—date from the last decade of the thirteenth century, all having Arnolfo di Cambio as their architect. Dante at this time was active in civic life, and a member of a circle of poets who by their sonnets and lyrics gave birth to Tuscan vernacular literature. The young Giotto had left his sheep-folds for Cimabue's studio, and had embarked on the first of his great series of frescoes—the life of St. Francis in the Upper Church at Assisi. From him, with his incomparable power of telling a story and his sense of human values, Italian painting took its rise. If the dawn of the Florentine Renaissance belongs to the age of Dante, another great leap forward was made at the turn of the fourteenth and fifteenth centuries. This was the age of humanism, when the classical revival opened out a new conception of life. Men were learning from Cicero the importance of the relationship between thought and action; the ideal philosopher was no longer to be a recluse, withdrawn from the world, but one who exercised himself in the duties of citizenship. Leonardo Bruni, Chancellor of the Florentine Republic (1411–44), helped by his Latin translations of the works of Aristotle and Plato to familiarize his contemporaries with Greek thought. At the same time the Greek language was becoming better known; it was said that Florence might be Athens, so frequently could Greek be heard spoken in the streets. The spirit of the Renaissance was also at work in the arts. It is visible in the frescoes of Masaccio, the sculpture of Donatello and Ghiberti, and in Brunelleschi's masterpiece of architecture, the dome of the Cathedral. All alike show the immense advance in technique made in the past hundred years, together with escape from convention, love of experiment and a new emphasis on the dignity and significance of man. The Medici were thus inheritors of a great tradition. Lorenzo was not the creator of the Florentine Renaissance, but he raised it to its culminating point. He played his part by active association with the cultural interests of a highly intellectual and artistic people, and perhaps most of all by his direction of the affairs of state in such a way as to provide, both within and without Florence, the conditions under which the arts of peace could flourish.

It is a fact of considerable significance that the Italian Renaissance had its origin in the independent city-state.

Everywhere the object of man's patriotic devotion was not Italy but his own city. This was his *patria*, for which he craved power, prosperity, fine buildings, citizens who could win fame by their talents and above all liberty. Each city thought of itself as the Roman Republic in miniature, where power lay with the sovereign people and its elected councils. Despots derived their authority in the first instance from the republic, which laid down the conditions under which they should rule, and exacted an oath of consent to them. When Jacopo Carrara was entrusted with the government of Padua, he was made to swear, among other things, to keep the city well supplied with food and to protect the University, and an annual sum was voted for his expenses. Such a contract is typical of those made between many despots and republics. The right of the people to confer power on a lord had as its corollary the right to withdraw it. Every despot was aware that in order to maintain his position he must satisfy the citizens that his rule was in their interests, and that his presence added lustre to the city. Thus whether the citizens continued to manage their own affairs or whether they yielded supreme power to one of their number, each city proved a fertile soil for the cultivation of the arts in a form which gave expression to the peculiar genius of its people.

The tendency of the republic was to rely more exclusively than the despot upon native talent. Duccio, a contemporary of Giotto, was the chief formative influence in Sienese art, and native painters continued for the next two centuries to work on the lines which he laid down "as if", says Berenson, "Florence were not forty but forty million miles away". They were masters of decorative art, as may be seen on the pavement of the Cathedral, where the designs which cover it date from the fourteenth to the nineteenth century. Their mysticism, passion for beauty and soft colouring enabled the Sienese to make a distinctive contribution to Renaissance painting. Yet, owing to their tendency to turn in upon themselves, inspiration was failing them by the end of the fifteenth century. It was an alien from Perugia—Pintoricchio—whom Cardinal Piccolomini employed to decorate the Cathedral Library at Siena with scenes from the life of his uncle, Pope Pius II. Pintoricchio and Perugino were both employed in various places outside their native city, among them in Rome, and under their leadership the Umbrian school of Perugia grew in fame. Thither came Raphael of Urbino to work in Perugino's studio. When he migrated to Florence he grafted all that the Florentines could teach him upon the Umbrian tradition which was the foundation of his art.

In no city does the Renaissance reflect more fully the temperament and ideals of a people than in Venice. The Republic of St. Mark was in the eyes of its citizens "the greatest and most glorious that the world has ever seen, that of Rome alone excepted". Confident in themselves and untroubled by political problems, their intent was to enjoy their heritage and to contribute to its splendour. A legacy from Cardinal Bessarion to the *Biblioteca Marciana* of 600 Greek manuscripts was an impetus to classical studies, but Venetian interests lay in language, history and literature rather than in philosophy. In the art of printing and glass-making, in the oriental richness of colour which distinguishes their painting, in everything, in short, which called for technical skill, the Venetians were supreme. The works of the leading Venetian painters—the Bellini brothers, Carpaccio, Giorgione, Titian, Veronese—alike show the serenity of a people at peace with themselves, and a unique power of giving pleasure to the eye. Their ideal of beauty is expressed in Giorgione's *Sleeping Venus*, where a superbly beautiful woman rests in a cave opening upon a lovely landscape. Great is the contrast between it and Botticelli's *Birth of Venus*, in which Venus poised on a shell, blown by the winds amid rippling waves, wonderingly anticipates the future, and all is light and movement. The differences between these two ideals of beauty sum up those which marked the character and history of the two chief cities of the Italian Renaissance.

Possession of supreme power gave to the despot greater opportunity to experiment and to bring new influences to bear on native scholars and artists by inviting men of other cities to work among them. All the chief cities had their universities and made ample provision for legal studies which were the gateway to a professional career. Republics, however, were slow in founding Chairs in the new humanistic subjects of Rhetoric and Poetry, of which the economic advantage was less apparent. It was largely through princes, or leading citizens of the Medici type, that the new learning was established in the universities. Ferrara was second only to Florence as a centre of humanistic studies owing to the invitation of its lord to Guarino of Verona in 1429 to undertake the education of his son. Guarino had worked in Greece under Chrysoloras and was the foremost teacher of his age. Leonello d'Este, the heir to Ferrara, became under his tutelage an accomplished scholar, and for the remainder of his life, Guarino held the Chair of Greek and Latin Letters in the University. Students from all parts of Europe flocked to Ferrara, to sit at Guarino's feet; among them was the little group of Englishmen, which included John Tiptoft, Earl of Worcester, and John Free, the poor scholar from Balliol. During the later years of the fifteenth century a pupil of Guarino held, under the patronage of the Bentivoglio, the Chair of Rhetoric and Poetry in that stronghold of legal studies, the University of Bologna. Here, too, the wish of Giovanni Bentivoglio that his children should be versed in "poetry, oratory and the liberal arts" brought humanists to the city as private tutors, who at the same time lectured in the University. Mantua and Urbino were small cities, possessed of scanty resources. Each were famous in the history of the Renaissance owing to the cultivated tastes of their rulers and the fortunes which they amassed as *condottiere* captains. Private wealth enabled the Gonzaga lords of Mantua to build their vast

Regia and to employ a succession of artists to decorate it, of which the first and greatest was Mantegna. In the little city of Urbino, high in the Apennines, the soldier scholar, Duke Federico da Montefeltro, founded the finest of fifteenth-century dwelling-places still in being today. Here he amassed a library of choice manuscripts, each book bound in crimson, ornamented with silver. His biographer, Vespasiano, compared its catalogue with those of other libraries—the Vatican, Florence, Venice, even with that of "the University of Oxford in England"—and found it superior to them all.

At the court of Lodovico Sforza, Duke of Milan, the glories of the Renaissance city-state reached their height. In the words of the contemporary historian Corio : "The court of our princes was most splendid, full of new fashions, new clothes and new pleasures. . . . Here shone the learning of the Greeks, and the poetry and prose of the Latins. Here the muses sang and the masters of sculpture and painting worked." The character of the Milanese Renaissance was to a greater degree than elsewhere determined by her rulers. Work on the two great buildings founded in the days of the Visconti, the Cathedral of Milan and the Certosa of Pavia, continued almost without intermission under the Sforza. To them was added their own monument—the Castello Sforzesco. All three became schools of architecture and sculpture in which local craftsmen gained fresh inspiration from masters such as Filarete the Florentine and Bramante of Urbino, brought thither by the Dukes. Lodovico attracted men of talent from all parts of Europe to his court, and kept Leonardo da Vinci in his service for some eighteen years. Leonardo was employed to design costumes for masques, to stage-manage tournaments, to decorate rooms in the Castello, to advise on town-planning and to make guns and bridges. Amidst these manifold activities he produced masterpieces of painting, among them the *Last Supper* and the *Virgin of the Rocks*, and every native artist set himself to paint in Leonardo's style. At no other time or place was life more civilized or more absorbing, but there were signs of a fatal weakness in the growing separation between court and city. Lodovico came to look upon his state as his private possession, as the field upon which his personality could express itself. He lost sight of the necessity for commending his rule to the people. Thus whilst the gay life of the court went on, discontent and faction raised their heads in the city unheeded. Partnership between prince and people was essential to the stability of the city-state and the hall-mark of the early Renaissance. Its break-up was the prelude to disaster. When in 1499 the armies of France descended upon Milan to claim the Duchy for Louis XII, the grandson of Valentina Visconti, they were led by Gian Giacomo Trivulzio, a malcontent Milanese. Resistance to the invader was unreliable and ineffective, and Lodovico ended his days in a French prison.

The foreign invasions of Italy marked the close of an epoch. Some city-states ceased to be independent; few were free to cultivate the arts of peace as, in spite of petty wars, they had been able to do for the past fifty years. Thus the phase of the early Renaissance ended, to be succeeded by that of the high Renaissance centred upon Rome, which reached its zenith under Leo X, the son of Lorenzo dei Medici. Leo built on the foundations laid by Julius II, who during the ten years of his pontificate (1503–13) worked feverishly to increase the power and prestige of the Papacy. As one means to this end, he resolved to make of Rome a splendid Renaissance capital. Bramante was made the Pope's architect-in-chief. He is responsible for the original design of the new St. Peter's, upon which others worked; he built the long galleries connecting the Vatican palace with the garden pavilion known as the Belvedere; he was employed on making new streets, dredging the Tiber, and building and repairing churches and palaces throughout the city. At Bramante's suggestion his fellow-townsman Raphael was set to work on the decoration of the Vatican *Stanze*, which Julius used as his private apartments. The first room to be finished expresses the humanist faith in the harmony between all forms of knowledge. Theology, in the fresco known as the *Disputa*, links the Church on earth with the Church in heaven. It is partnered by the *School of Athens*, in which Plato and Aristotle preside over a great company of philosophers. The promulgators of the Civil and the Canon Law face Apollo and the Muses, surrounded by the poets of all ages. Thus the walls of truth and beauty stand four-square.

Michelangelo made up the triumvirate of genius in the Pope's service, dividing his time between covering the ceiling of the Sistine Chapel with frescoes and working on the colossal tomb designed to perpetuate Julius II's memory, of which only a fragment survives. Julius was fortunate in his collaborators, and owing to his energy and driving power great things were accomplished in a short time. Yet he was not himself a connoisseur of the arts. His successor was steeped from childhood in the spirit of the Renaissance. A youth spent in Florence had fostered in Giovanni dei Medici both love of learning and artistic perception. His elevation to the Papacy gave him an opportunity to indulge his tastes, and Rome during his pontificate became a paradise for scholars and artists. For his confidential secretaries he chose two distinguished Latinists, Sadoleto and the Venetian Pietro Bembo; his first creation of cardinals included his friend and one-time tutor Bernardo Bibbiena; Castiglione, who was in Rome as the representative of the Duke of Urbino, continued to enjoy papal favour after his master had been expelled from his Duchy. Among the artists, Michelangelo and Raphael continued in active work, Leonardo da Vinci migrated to Rome, and was installed in apartments in the Belvedere. Sebastiano del Piombo came from Venice and Sodoma from Siena, whilst the one native artist of note, Giulio Romano, was Raphael's disciple. The mingling of representatives of many local traditions, together with the touch of universality gained from their presence in Rome and their study of ancient models, combined to produce an art which was in the widest sense Italian.

The outstanding figure in the brilliant society which Leo X gathered round him was Raphael. During his short life he came under the influence of all the leading schools of Italian painting and, with his great receptive power, made their distinctive qualities his own. He was the much-loved friend of the humanists, whose ideas he absorbed and expressed in his art. After Bramante's death he was placed in charge of the work at St. Peter's, and also appointed inspector of antiquities in Rome. The fruit of his archæological studies may be seen in his own work —notably in the decoration of the Vatican *Loggie*. His artistic output was phenomenal, including as it did the continuation of his work in the *Stanze*, designs for tapestries to hang in the Sistine Chapel,[1] the Madonna di San Sisto, portraits of Leo X, Castiglione, Bibbiena and other leading humanists, and the decoration of the *Farnesina*, the villa owned by the banker Agostino Chigi on the banks of the Tiber. The orders which poured in on him were beyond the power of any one man to execute, and much of the work was left to his pupils. Yet all that he planned or touched was inspired by "a certain ideal that is in my mind", as he wrote in a letter to a friend. It was an ideal of beauty and of joy in life for which he strove alike in his Madonnas and in his *Galatea* driving her dolphins through the waves at the Farnesina.

The Pope himself was the moving spirit in every activity of the Rome of his day. True to the habits in which he had been brought up, he was punctilious in the performance of his religious duties. Both the matter and the manner of sermons preached in his presence came under his scrutiny, and he made it a rule that none should last longer than a quarter of an hour. The perfection of the papal choir, for which singers were brought from

[1] Some of these cartoons were bought by Charles I and are now in the South Kensington Museum.

many lands, owed much to his delight in music. New buildings and new works of art were, on his initiative, added daily to the splendours of Rome. The literary atmosphere of the Vatican was fostered by the patronage bestowed on poets, by learned discussions which took place in the Pope's company, and by fresh accessions to the library. Scholars dedicated their works to him, thereby, as he wrote in a letter of thanks, conferring immortality upon him. With no less zest did the Pope participate in the revels of the Carnival, with its masquerades, plays and dances. He enjoyed a day's hunting, an evening game of cards or a banquet given by Agostino Chigi in the open loggia of his villa, where Raphael's frescoes added charm to the feast. True Medici that he was, he collected the members of his family around him and worked persistently for their advancement. Life in the Rome of Leo X was that of Medicean Florence on a grand scale.

In the opinion of his times Leo X's reign was both popular and successful. His aim was to please and be pleased, and he handled the diplomatic situation in Italy with considerable skill. He was fortunate in that he did not live to see Italy become the battlefield between Francis I and Charles V. It was the fate of the second Medici Pope to experience the full horrors of foreign invasion, when for three days, in May 1527, Rome was plundered by greedy and fanatical German and Spanish soldiers. The sack of Rome marked the end of the Italian Renaissance. Some of the leading figures of the age, such as Leonardo and Raphael, had been dead for several years; now scholars and artists were dispersed, and irreparable loss was suffered through the destruction of books, manuscripts, bronzes, marbles and other treasures. More important was the disillusionment which spread among Italians as they realized their helplessness in the face of their invaders. The confidence of the humanists was shattered, and man seemed no longer the master of his destiny but the sport of fortune. As at other times of crisis, men's thoughts turned towards religion for a way of escape from present troubles. Leo X thought that he had disposed of Luther by ordering his writings to be burned, but Luther's teaching on faith in the saving power of God attracted the attention of many educated Italians and changed their outlook on life. The theme of Michelangelo's *Last Judgment*, which he painted in the Sistine Chapel after the sack of Rome, is the greatness of God and the nothingness of man. A poem written in his later years shows the extent to which faith in his own creative powers had yielded to faith in God.

Nè pinger, nè scolpir fie più che quieti
L'anima volta a quel amor divina
C'aperse a prender noi in croce le braccia.[1]

For a time it seemed that men imbued with the spirit of the Renaissance would effect a revival of religion and a reform of abuses in the Church which would satisfy the aspirations of the age. But the violence of the extremists and the fears of the orthodox divided Christendom into two warring camps, and the way of reconciliation was abandoned for that of repression. In the Italy of the Counter-Reformation, free expression of opinion, such as had marked the proceedings of the Platonic Academy, was no longer tolerated. Heretics were burned, printing was rigidly censored and draperies were added to the splendid nude figures of Michelangelo's *Last Judgment* for the sake of decorum. By the middle of the sixteenth century Spanish domination in Italy was an accomplished fact, and Spanish influence was everywhere a deterrent to energy and initiative. In a few places Renaissance civilization survived for a time. Ferrara was not brought under the direct rule of the Papacy until the end of the century, and in the service of the Este Dukes first Ariosto and then Tasso raised Italian poetry to the

[1] "Neither painting nor sculpture can give rest to the soul, which turns to Divine Love, opening His arms to us on the Cross."

height of its beauty. Venice remained the freest and most prosperous state in Italy, where scholars pursued by the Inquisition found asylum and great works of art continued to be produced. Elsewhere the spirit of the Renaissance was crushed under the double weight of Spain and the Counter-Reformation. Even in cities such as Florence, which retained their native rulers, much of the old free tradition was destroyed through the impact of stiff Spanish manners and the emphasis laid upon class distinctions.

Meanwhile, beyond the Alps Renaissance Italy conquered her conquerors. The French returned home to refashion the setting of their lives on the model which they had learned to admire in Italy. Francis I brought Leonardo da Vinci back with him to France where he spent the last years of his life as an honoured guest. Italian painters were employed to decorate Fontainebleau, and royal lectureships were founded in Greek and other humanistic studies. The King's aim was to become, by the cultivation of his manifold gifts, a perfect example of a Renaissance prince. Among the Frenchmen who had been most active in Italy were Cardinal d'Amboise and his soldier brother. Their Château of Gaillon in Normandy ranks among the examples of the transformation in French architecture effected by the lightening and enriching of the work of native master-masons by Italian decoration. Italian influences penetrated into England, partly through French channels and even more through English visitors to Italy. Thomas Linacre, the complete humanist, learned in all branches of knowledge, came under the direct influence of the Florentine Renaissance. Poliziano was his guide to the classics, and in later years he dedicated his edition of Galen to Leo X, in memory of the medical studies which they pursued together in Florence. Linacre's pupil, John Colet, also went to Florence; both his educational ideals and his lectures on St. Paul's epistles bear the imprint of Marsilio Ficino's influence. To the part played by Englishmen in Italy, and Italians in England, in the dissemination of Italian culture must be added the progress of printing in Italy, which led to the rapid circulation of Italian books. Castiglione's *Courtier* was known in England two years after it was published by the Aldine Press in Venice, and in the same year that Sir Thomas Hoby, the author of the English translation, was born. There were many educated Englishmen, statesmen as well as scholars, who both read and spoke Italian. In the era of the Reformation numerous voices were raised in condemnation of the corrupt morals of the Italians. The verdict of Roger Ascham, author of the *Scholemaster*, was that out of Italy came "plenty of new mischiefs, never known in England before". Nevertheless, Italy remained the chief standard of appeal in matters intellectual and artistic.

The Italian Renaissance, the fruit of Italy's past, stood for a new outlook upon life which made its influence felt throughout the civilized world. New belief in the dignity and power of man and his capacity for creative achievement, new interest in the world as the field of his conquests were visible in the upsurge of energy which distinguished Tudor England no less than fifteenth-century Florence. When the course of events pressed home the hard lesson of man's fallibility, the high hopes of those who believed that they had found the solution of life's problems were rudely shattered, yet faith in the spirit of man was not extinguished. The incentive to adventure remained strong and humanistic influence was widespread in the importance attached to learning as an equipment for life. The scholar no longer belonged to a class apart, immersed in his own studies and despised by men of birth as a clerk. A classical education, ability to write and speak in a way that carried conviction, knowledge of music and appreciation of the visual arts, came to be regarded as appropriate and even necessary in the soldier and the statesman. Of all the fruits of the Renaissance, perhaps the most enduring was the cult of beauty. Beauty, whether in nature, in art or in the adjuncts of domestic life, was venerated as never before. The garden pavilions erected in the grounds of great English houses in the sixteenth and seventeenth centuries are offsprings of the Renaissance ideal of the Platonic banquet in which choice food and wines were served in elegant vessels amid lovely surroundings, the whole designed to act as an incentive to philosophic discussion. The sense of beauty was the soul of the Italian Renaissance.

Short Bibliography

BIOGRAPHIES OF LORENZO DEI MEDICI

FABRONI, A.: *Laurentii Medicis Vita*, 2 vols., Pisa, 1784. Includes a useful appendix of letters.

ROSCOE, W.: *The Life of Lorenzo de' Medici*, 1796, 10th ed., Bohn's Standard Library, 1895.

VON REUMONT, A.: *Lorenzo dei Medici*, Eng. trans., Harrison, 1876.

ARMSTRONG, E.: *Lorenzo de' Medici* (Heroes of the Nations Series, 1896). Still the best general account of Lorenzo and the Florence of his day.

HORSBURGH, E. L. S.: *Lorenzo the Magnificent*, Methuen, 1905. Useful especially for detailed criticism of Lorenzo's poetry.

ROSS, J.: *Lives of the early Medici as told in their Correspondence*, Chatto & Windus, 1910. Very valuable for English readers.

PIERACCINI, G.: *La stirpe de' Medici di Cafaggiolo*, Vol. I, Florence, 1924. A family history, which discusses the physical and mental characteristics of each member, by an historian who is also a doctor.

FLORENTINE HISTORIES

HYETT, F. A.: *Florence, her History and her Art*, 1913.

SCHEVILL, F.: *History of Florence* (illustrated), Bell, 1937.

BOOKS ON SPECIAL SUBJECTS

BERENSON, B.: *Italian Painters of the Renaissance* (new illustrated edition), Phaidon Press, 1952.

CARTWRIGHT, J.: *The Painters of Florence*, Murray, 1900.

HORNE, H. P.: *Botticelli*, 1908.

ROBB, N.: *The Neoplatonism of the Italian Renaissance*, Allen & Unwin, 1935.

GRUNZWEIG: *Correspondence de la filiale de Bruges des Medici*, Pt. I, Brussels, 1931. An interesting picture of the working of a Medici bank.

RAYMOND DE ROOVER: *The Medici Bank*, O.U.P., 1948. A foretaste of the author's researches in the subject.

EINSTEIN, L.: *The Italian Renaissance in England*, Macmillan, 1902.

SYMONDS, J. A.: *Renaissance in Italy*, and BURCKHARDT, J.: *The Civilization of the Renaissance in Italy*, are classics of the mid-nineteenth century which still retain their value.

LORENZO DEI MEDICI: *Opere* (ed. Simioni; 2 vols.), Bari, 1913.

Index

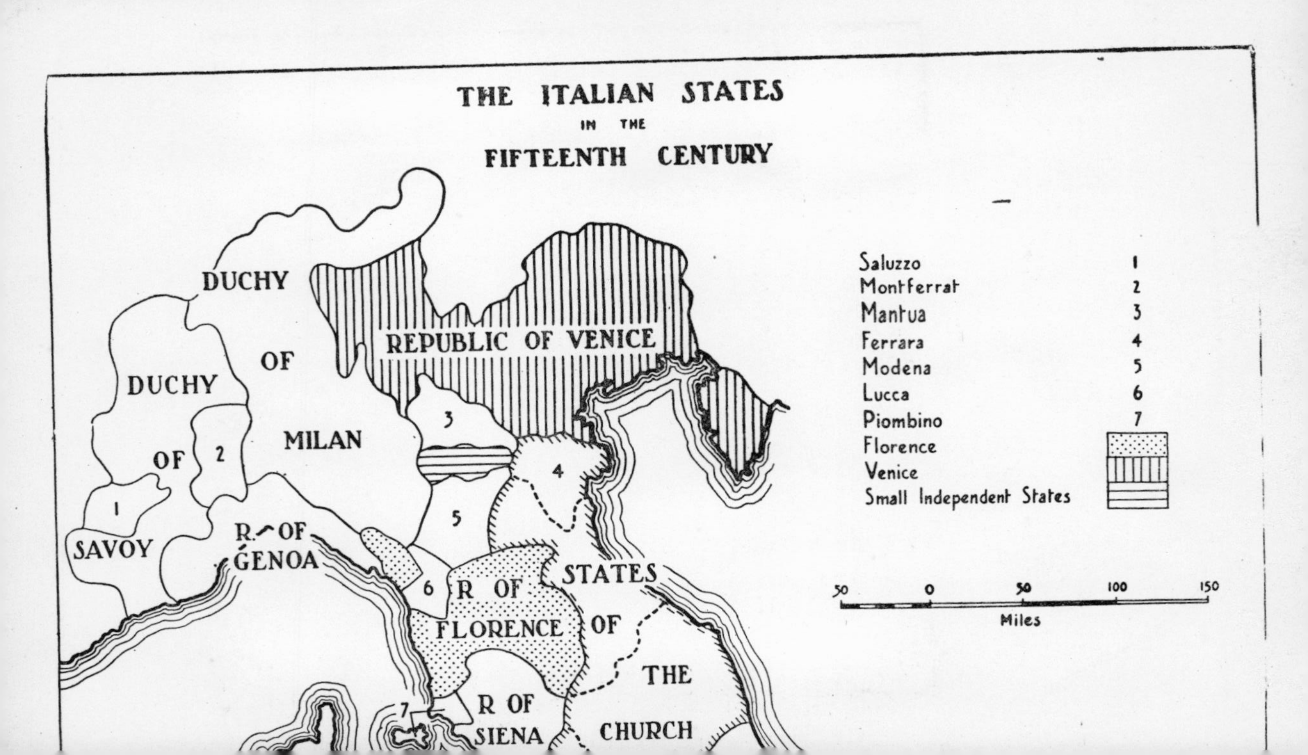
THE ITALIAN STATES
IN THE
FIFTEENTH CENTURY
DUCHY OF MILAN
DUCHY OF SAVOY
REPUBLIC OF VENICE
R. OF GENOA
R OF FLORENCE
R OF SIENA
STATES OF THE CHURCH
1
2
3
4
5
6
7
Saluzzo 1
Montferrat 2
Mantua 3
Ferrara 4
Modena 5
Lucca 6
Piombino 7
Florence
Venice
Small Independent States
50 0 50 100 150
Miles

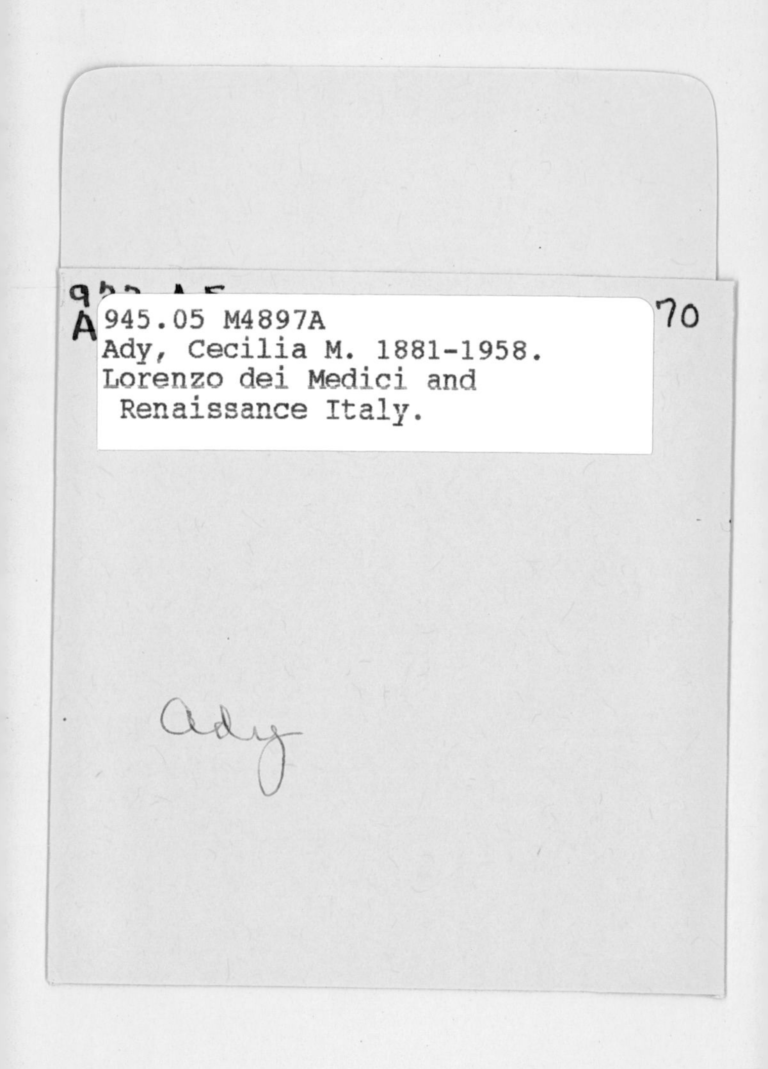
945.05 M4897A
Ady, Cecilia M. 1881-1958.
Lorenzo dei Medici and
Renaissance Italy.
70
Ady